CUT YOUR
ENERGY BILLS
N⚡W

CUT YOUR ENERGY BILLS NOW

150 Smart Ways to
SAVE MONEY & Make
Your Home More
COMFORTABLE & GREEN

BRUCE HARLEY

The Taunton Press

The Taunton Press
Inspiration for hands-on living®

The Taunton Press, Inc., 63 South Main Street, PO Box 5506, Newtown, CT 06470-5506
e-mail: tp@taunton.com

Editor: Steve Culpepper
Copy editor: Betty Christiansen
Indexer: James Curtis
Jacket/Cover design: Jean-Marc Troadec, Design & Typography
Interior design: Susan Fazekas
Layout: Kimberly Shake
Illustrator: Christine Erikson
Cover Photographer: Lauren Nicole/Photodisc/Getty Images
Photographer: Paul Anthony

Library of Congress Cataloging-in-Publication Data
Harley, Bruce, 1964-
   Cut your energy bills now : 150 smart ways to save money and make your home more comfortable and green /
Bruce Harley.
       p. cm.
   Includes bibliographical references and index.
   ISBN 978-1-60085-070-7 (alk. paper)
   1. Dwellings--Energy conservation--Amateurs' manuals. 2. Dwellings--Maintenance and repair--Amateurs'
manuals. 3. Sustainable living--Amateurs' manuals. I. Title.
   TJ163.5.D86H37 2008
   644--dc22
                        2008033594

Printed in the United States of America
10 9 8 7 6 5 4 3 2 1

TRADEMARKS

3M®, Aeroseal®, Air Conditioning Contractors of America® (ACCA), Airetrak™, AirGenerate™, AirTap™, Autocirc1®
(Laing), Allied Window®, Bi-Glass®, Bosch®, CertainTeed®, Cityproof®, CPFilms®, DELTA®-FL, Dow® Thermax™,
Dumpster®, EcoOption™, ENERGY STAR®, GE®, Grundfos®, Hampton Bay®, Harvey®, Innerglass® Window
Systems, Kill A Watt™, Mac®, Metlund® D'MAND®, Microsoft® Windows®, Noritz®, ODL®, Owens Corning®,
PowerCost Monitor™, Q-Lon®, RESNETˢᴹ, Rinnai®, Skyview®, Smart Strip®, Solar Rating & Certification
Corporationˢᴹ, Solatube®, Sun-Dome®, Sun-Tek®, SunPipe®, Taco®, Takagi, TED® The Energy Detective™, Teflon®,
Typar®, Tyvek®, Tyz-All™, Uponorˢᴹ, Velcro®, Velux®, Venmar®, Vise-Grip®, Wattson®.

To Kenja.
I hope that we'll leave you a world
that's better than we found it.

Acknowledgments

Many thanks to:

Steve Cowell, Kathleen DeVito, Mark Dyen, Jim Fitzgerald, Shirley Harris, Adam Parker, David Weitz, and the Building Science and Corporate Communications teams at Conservation Services Group for support on all levels. Michael Blasnik, M. Blasnik & Associates. Terry Brennan, Camroden Associates. Heather Clark, WinnDevelopment. Jim Conachen, Bi-Glass. Chris Derby-Kilfoyle, Berkshire Photovoltaic Systems, Rick Duncan, Honeywell. Philip Fairey, Neil Moyer, and Sherri Shields, Florida Solar Energy Center. Heather Ferrier, Ferrier Custom Builders. John Garrity, Patrick McElhaney, and Jeffrey Renaud, General Electric. Adam Gifford, Conservation Services Group. Jon Haehnel, Building Envelope Solutions, Inc. Tom Herron and Cheryl Gendron, National Fenestration Rating Council. Aaron Hill, Suntrek Industries. Stephen M. Hill, AirTight Insulation. Martin Holladay, Energy Design Update. Bill Hulstrunk, National Fiber. Paul Lipke, Sustainable Step New England. Bret Monroe, Monroe Infrared Technology, Inc. John O'Connell and Mike Pierce, Energy Federation. Ken Neuhauser, Building Science Corporation. Dana VanBlair, Jandy. Chandler von Schrader, Jonathan Passe at EPA. Barb Yankie, Homes +, Inc. Kathie Zehnder, Power Creative.

To all the building science people, the builders and subs I've worked with, the architects and designers and building officials: You all have taught and inspired me over the years.

To Eric Jackson and Torben Gundtofte-Bruun, for last-minute help with keyboards, and Molly Kerns, Tsubo Massage, for keeping me going.

To the Taunton folks who let us loose in their homes, and to Steve Culpepper and Courtney Jordan for keeping me on track.

To Mieke and Kenja for support (as well as tolerance), through thick and thin.

To Carol, Paula, Briana, Dave, Barb, Vanda, Karen, Roland, Elise, Chris, and Eleanor, for help and support in countless ways throughout the process.

And to my parents, Bob and Barbara, who taught me all the really important stuff.

Contents

CHAPTER 1

Plan Your Energy Fixes

In this book, we'll show you more than 150 ways to save energy in your home. Some are easy, some are difficult. Some you can do yourself; others you'll need professional help to get done.

The goal is to steer you toward value by focusing on steps that are low cost or high benefit; some are both. For those projects you'll do yourself, I offer tools and tips from 18 years of direct experience in helping people save energy and improve comfort. For those projects that need outside help, I'll teach you what to look for in a contractor, what to ask him or her to do, and what to expect. Some steps aren't projects at all, but simply ask you to pay a bit more attention, by smart shopping, planning ahead, or making yourself more aware of your day-to-day use of the energy-consuming "stuff" in your home.

What to tackle first? Every house is different, and so is every family, so there's no recipe for the "right" solution. Before we start looking at the projects themselves, we'll talk about the house as a series of systems, and the ways these systems use energy. Understanding your energy use will help you create a strategy that works for you and will help you capitalize on opportunities to reduce costs or leverage benefits whenever you are doing other remodeling work on your house. I'll provide an overview of environmental impact and health and safety concerns right in your home. Then I'll show you how to get outside help when you need it: financial help, technical help, and contractor help. This will help you plan ahead so you can get the maximum benefit from these steps and projects at a minimum cost and effort.

tip Your house is a system. The systems in your house are supposed to work together to provide you with a safe, comfortable place to live. When the entire system is working properly, each smaller system makes its contribution, but when one component doesn't do its job, it can throw off the entire system. That can affect your energy bills, as well as your comfort, health, safety, and home maintenance bills.

◄ Increasing the energy efficiency of your house can be as involved as installing a solar water heater, or as simple as sealing windows and doors with weatherstripping. (Photo by Brian Vanden Brink courtesy *Fine Homebuilding* magazine.)

Think of Your House as One Big System

tip **What are we buying?** Most of us would like to see our energy bills go away, but we don't spend that much time thinking about them. At the end of the month, we are not proud owners of kilowatt-hours and therms; we pay for the comfort and utility we enjoy in our homes. We pay to keep warm in winter, to keep cool in summer, and to have hot running water. We pay for our toast and coffee, our TV and computer, our answering machine and cell phone charger. *Conservation* implies sacrifice, or at least a willingness to get by with a little less. *Efficiency* means enjoying the same level of comfort and convenience using less energy. Conservation usually costs nothing; efficiency typically involves an investment. There is a place for both approaches in any effort to save energy, carbon, and money, but the focus of this book is on *efficiency* in the house system.

Your house is a machine for living; a big system made of smaller systems. Each plays its part in the performance of the whole; each affects your well-being. Heating, cooling, lighting, layout, and the flow of air and moisture all impact your comfort, health, energy use, and cash flow.

The system can be complex, but consider this simple example: One person in the house regularly bumps the thermostat up a couple of degrees, and another person pushes it back down. Sound familiar? The changes in the thermostat tell the heating or cooling system to turn on or shut off, which has an immediate impact on temperature and comfort, as well as air and moisture flow and energy use.

People's perceptions of comfort affect their actions. Yet perceptions are only the tip of the iceberg. In this chapter, I explain the main systems we'll be considering in this book: electrical systems, heating, cooling, water heating, the building enclosure, and a few of the ways that things can go wrong.

1 UNDERSTAND YOUR ENERGY COSTS

In 2007, the average household spent between $2,100 and $2,500 a year on energy, and costs are rising. (This does not include gasoline for automobiles, yard care, or recreation.)

Those dollars are split about equally between electricity and gas, although for homes using oil for heat, costs are higher—and rising more quickly—than for homes heated with gas. Most analysts agree that energy costs will continue to rise steadily as worldwide demand continues to increase and supplies of fossil fuels tighten.

Energy Expenses by Use—Average per Home

This chart shows the annual expenses, divided by general categories of use, for the average American home in cold and hot climates. Although the heating and cooling consumption varies, both the total amounts and the relative sizes of the other categories are surprisingly steady across climates.

■ Heating
■ Air-Conditioning
■ Water Heating
■ Refrigerators
■ Other Appliances & Lights

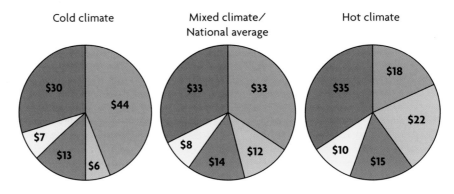

Cold climate: $30, $44, $7, $13, $6

Mixed climate/National average: $33, $33, $8, $14, $12

Hot climate: $35, $18, $22, $10, $15

The House as a System

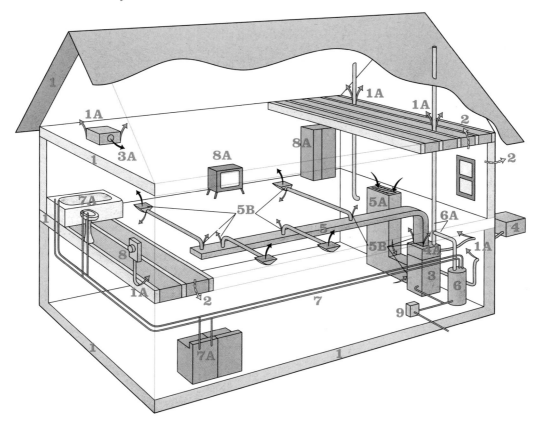

1 The walls, roof, and foundation form the enclosure, or *thermal boundary*, of the house. Their job is to separate indoors from outdoors, keeping out heat, cold, wind, water, pests, and intruders.

1A Holes in the enclosure create pathways for air, allowing heat or cooling to escape and pests to enter. They can also create paths for the rapid spread of fire, and for moisture to get out or in, where it can condense and cause trouble.

2 Insulation is typically installed in wall cavities, attics, and floors to reduce heat movement (out in the winter and in during the summer). Gaps in insulation allow heat to flow in or out—even where no air is leaking. Cold spots from insulation gaps can create condensation that leads to mold growth.

3 Your heating and cooling systems should maintain comfortable temperatures. The heat is usually supplied by burning gas, although it may be oil, propane, or electric; air conditioners run on electricity.

3A Bathroom and other exhaust fans can compete with a natural-draft furnace or water heater for indoor air; a bathroom fan can dump moisture into the attic.

4 Air conditioners use an outdoor coil or compressor to dump unwanted heat outdoors.

4A The cooling coil (or evaporator) is usually a separate unit mounted in the duct next to your furnace.

5 Supply ducts bring heated or cooled air into the home. Some homes use pipes and radiators, instead of ducts.

5A The return duct(s) bring house air back to the system to be heated or cooled.

5B Holes in ducts let hot or cold air out of the house, reducing comfort and efficiency. These leaks also change the pressure in your home, bringing in soil gases or mold from your basement or carbon monoxide from your garage or heating system, causing ice dams or moisture damage.

6 Your water heater may be powered by gas, electricity, oil, or propane. It may be wasting energy even when you aren't using hot water.

6A Your water heater or furnace vent system can leak combustion gases, including deadly carbon monoxide, because of air pressures in the house created by exhaust fans or your furnace fan.

7 Plumbing pipes bring hot and cold water to your plumbing fixtures. The fixtures, and the way you use hot water, consume energy.

8 Your electrical system includes a meter, circuit breakers, and wires to bring electricity to lights, appliances, and outlets. It doesn't use electricity; it only carries it where it's needed.

8A Large and small appliances use electricity when you are operating them, and sometimes when you aren't.

9 Your fuel supply system consists of a gas meter and pipes. Like the electrical system, it doesn't use gas; it only supplies fuel where it's needed. If you use oil or propane, it is stored in a tank on your property.

How Much Can You Save?

The energy business is full of good news and bad news. The bad news is that your energy usage is probably high; the good news is that there's potential for real savings. The more you've been using, the more you can save.

How much might you save over time? We'll look at several major factors that influence your savings so you can get an idea. If you want more detailed estimates of savings customized for your house, climate, and past history, a professional energy assessment can guide you.

In most homes, the highest monthly gas bill in the winter is a rough estimate of potential yearly heating savings, for reasonably cost-effective measures, but if your use is very high, you may do better. Your electricity savings could be anywhere from 10 percent to 40 percent of your electric bill, depending on where you start and how far you want to go.

The age of your house is also a big factor. On average, houses built before 1950 use more energy than those from more recent time periods. Older homes weren't well insulated, and they are more likely to have older, less efficient equipment and appliances. But if your home was built more recently, even within the last few years, there may still be big opportunities for savings. Newer homes are less likely to need wall insulation, windows, or appliance upgrades, but they are equally likely to need air sealing and duct repairs.

▲ The EPA and U.S. Department of Energy jointly maintain a website that provides comprehensive information about all the ENERGY STAR programs (www.energystar.gov). See the "Home Improvement" and "Products" sections for the latest information and listings for your home energy needs.

2 SEPARATE YOUR ENERGY USES

A helpful way to understand your energy use is to compare yours to national averages. It's also helpful to estimate how much you spend on heating, cooling, water heating, and "other" (mostly lighting and appliances). Though inexact, it may help you find a particular area where you're unknowingly wasting a lot. (Note: a home-performance professional or auditor can help with this process; see p. 11.)

Here's how to do it:

1 First, gather your electricity and gas bills from the previous year. If you didn't save them, many monthly bills have a summary of the previous year's use. If yours doesn't, request that information from your utility company.

2 Total all the bills (electricity and gas or oil) for the past year, and divide that by the square footage of your house. Compare the total annual energy cost per square foot to the values in the top chart on the facing page. If you use a lot more energy than average, your potential for energy savings is high.

3 Separate your energy use by category. To do this, you need to know what fuel you use for what purpose. Most homes use natural gas for home heating and hot water, and electricity for cooling and "other"—lighting and appliances.

4 Estimate heating and cooling usage by calculating a "baseline" usage for gas and electricity. Find the lowest months of the year, and take their average. Multiply by 12 to get the annual baseline.

5 If you heat with gas, subtract your gas baseline from the total annual gas bill—that's what you spend on heating (if you have a gas-fired pool heater, you may have a gas usage peak in the summer as well).

6 Do the same for electricity to get your air-conditioning use; if you have a pool, the increased summer usage would also include the pool pump. Your electricity baseline is typically refrigeration, lighting, and appliances.

7 You may have an increased electricity load in winter, due to higher lighting use, furnace fan operation, or electric heating. In that case, subtract the baseline from the totals of summer and winter months separately. Note that your water heater, oven/range, or dryer may each run on either gas or electricity.

8 Compare the totals to the chart on p. 4 to gauge your use for each of these general categories.

Average Household Energy Costs in Dollars per Square Foot

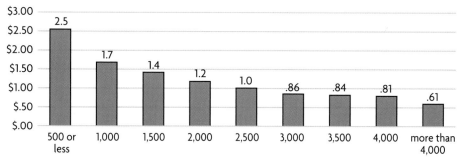

In the example, the total annual bill is $2,700, and the space—a large apartment—is 3,800 sq. ft. The annual energy cost for this apartment is $.71 per square foot, actually a bit lower than the national average for its size.

Baseline vs. Heating Gas Usage

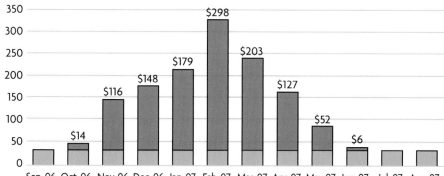

The light green section of the graph shows the baseline use; the dark green shows the remainder, which is for heating. Note that the bill dates are later than the month the energy was consumed. The baseline for this year of gas bills is $32. That's about $372 for cooking and hot water—the other gas uses in the home—higher than the average of $288. The remainder, $1,140, is what this household used for heating; that's also a bit higher than the average of $963 for a cold climate.

Bill Date	Therms	Payment
9/13/06	13	$33
10/12/06	21	$47
11/14/06	84	$148
12/12/06	102	$180
1/11/07	124	$211
2/12/07	218	$330
3/12/07	166	$236
4/11/07	105	$159
5/10/07	49	$85
6/10/07	18	$38
7/12/07	15	$34
8/13/07	13	$31
Total	929	$1531

Baseline vs. Cooling Electric Usage

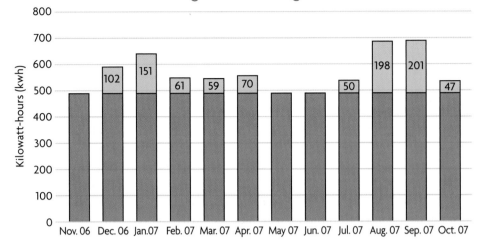

The baseline for this electric bill is the average of November, May, and June use: 489 kwh. That's 5,880 kwh per year, or about $91 per month and $1,092 per year. This is higher than the cold climate average of $809 for refrigeration, lights, and appliances, but not dramatically. Note that there is a winter increase and a summer increase: The winter increase, a total of 445 kwh, or $87 for November to April, is most likely the furnace fan and increased lighting use during the darker months. The summer increase of 497 kwh, or $80 for July to October, is from air-conditioning; it's well below the cold-climate average of $133.

Bill Date	kWh	Payment
11/13/06	496	$92
12/14/06	591	$103
1/17/07	640	$113
2/14/07	550	$109
3/16/07	548	$108
4/16/07	559	$110
5/15/07	497	$94
6/14/07	473	$87
7/16/07	539	$98
8/14/07	687	$123
9/13/07	690	$124
10/13/07	536	$99
Total	6310	$1169

Carbon Emissions of Common Household Fuels

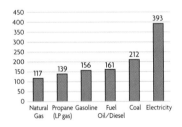

Natural gas emits the least carbon per unit of the common fossil fuels; coal has the most. Electricity (national average) has the highest greenhouse gas impact: First, because conventional power plants are inherently inefficient, and second, because of the high carbon content of coal, which fuels about half our electric generation.

Your Home's Environmental Impact

Your house and energy use affect the environment in two major ways. In the big picture, energy consumed is responsible for greenhouse gas emissions, such as carbon. There are also many secondary effects, such as the environmental consequences of land use, transportation to and from home, wastewater treatment, and household waste disposal. Closer to home, we'll consider how your house systems affect the indoor environment, and their direct impacts on you and your family.

3 THE CARBON IMPACT

Energy use in buildings is responsible for 40 percent of the country's carbon emissions, which is slightly more than those from transportation. Homes contribute about half of that, and energy use is the culprit.

In most homes, heating and cooling are the biggest energy users. But electricity has the highest carbon emissions—almost 3.5 times that of natural gas (see the chart at left). So if your first concern is climate change, focus on electricity savings: lighting and appliances, air-conditioning, and other electricity uses. You probably can't get to zero, but you can buy green power or carbon offsets for what you do use (see "Buy Green Power" on p. 11).

4 THE HEALTH IMPACT

Moisture in homes is a contributing factor to respiratory ailments and allergies. Studies by the Environmental Protection Agency (EPA) estimate that more than 20 percent of asthma cases in the United States are attributable to dampness and mold exposure in buildings, costing the health care system (and all of us) $3.5 billion annually.

How does your house affect your health? Control of heat- and airflow in buildings has a strong connection to moisture. This includes controlling condensation and humidity, along with repair of plumbing leaks, roof leaks, and water leaks in walls, as well as controlling moisture in basements. Movement of air can help dry things out, but it can also introduce moisture, which makes controlling airflow important.

Other health concerns include combustion gases and deadly carbon monoxide that can be produced by furnaces, water heaters, ovens, and cars. Air pressures created in homes by the furnace fan and ductwork can draw these gases into the home. Energy efficiency is often wrongly blamed for air quality problems. Efficiency work can indeed cause trouble if implemented carelessly, but when tackled with a systems approach, efficiency strategies can improve your health by effectively controlling heat, air, and moisture.

Carbon Emissions of Electricity by Region

- 130
- 300
- 400–450
- 450–500

Where you live makes a big difference in the carbon emissions of your electric supply. On the Pacific coast, emissions are nearly equal to natural gas, due to the large proportion of hydroelectric and renewable power. The central Midwest has the highest, due to heavy dependence on coal.

▲ A fan like this is the only fresh-air ventilation system in most homes, but the average bathroom fan is noisy, moves little or no air, and runs less than an hour a day. See p. 34 for tips on improving fresh air and controlling moisture in your home. (Photo by John Curtis)

▲ Every home should have at least one carbon monoxide detector. Follow the manufacturer's recommendations for number and placement. (Photo courtesy Kidde.)

◀ Warm, moist air from the house can leak into attics or other cold areas and condense on structural components, leading to rot and mold. Sealing leaks and controlling humidity will reduce or stop this unwanted moisture. (Photo by Steven Smulski, courtesy *Fine Homebuilding* magazine, © The Taunton Press, Inc.)

Unwanted Moisture Comes from Inside and Outside

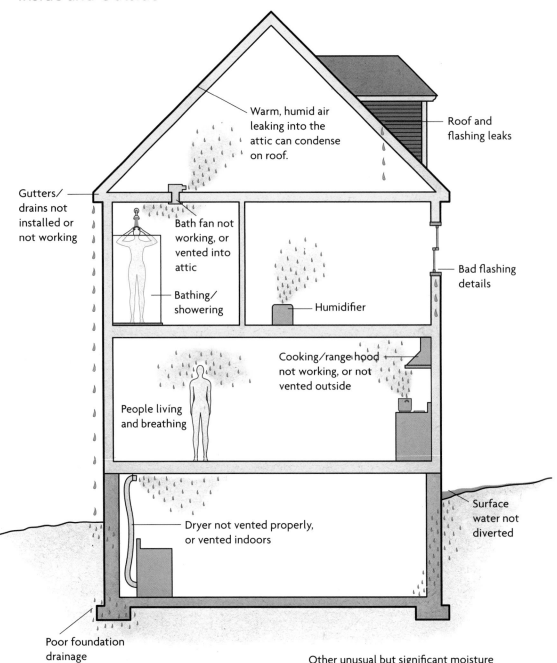

Warm, humid air leaking into the attic can condense on roof.

Roof and flashing leaks

Gutters/ drains not installed or not working

Bath fan not working, or vented into attic

Bathing/ showering

Humidifier

Bad flashing details

Cooking/range hood not working, or not vented outside

People living and breathing

Dryer not vented properly, or vented indoors

Surface water not diverted

Poor foundation drainage

Other unusual but significant moisture sources include drying firewood, uncovered tropical fish tanks, or attached greenhouses.

Getting Some Help

Chances are, as you go through this book and consider all the projects, you may not know where to start. You'll find that some projects are too involved to tackle right away. They may take more time, knowledge, technical ability, or funding than you have available right now. Or you may have a special situation that's not covered here. The good news is that you can get help in several areas: knowledge, implementation, and funding.

5 GET KNOWLEDGEABLE HELP

Despite all the good advice in this book, consider having a professional assessment of your home. Typically called "energy auditors," these pros assess your home's structure, equipment, lighting, and appliances, as well as your lifestyle, to account for where and how the energy is being used. Then the auditor can make specific recommendations for improvements, based on your actual situation.

Historically, utility company audits have been a cursory walk-through, with minimal awareness of the house as a system and limited opportunities for follow-through. You want a consultant who understands the house as a system, brings awareness of related health and safety issues, and can help you strategize your improvement opportunities.

Before hiring an auditor, ask what services he or she provides. Quality auditors will spend several hours in your home, looking carefully in your attic and basement and at your heating and cooling equipment and ductwork. They should perform

6 go green

BUY GREEN POWER

In many areas of the United States, you can purchase green power directly from your electric utility. When you choose the green option, the electric company collects a premium that contributes to a fund that may invest in new solar, wind, small hydro (hydroelectric), or other green electric generation. In that way, your power company can guarantee that the equivalent energy units that you use will be generated somewhere nearby and contribute to the electric grid. Some utilities offer more green power options. If you can't buy green power through your local utility, you can still purchase equivalent green energy credits through a number of organizations (see Resources on p. 116).

◄ A blower door is a large fan that depressurizes the home and measures the air leaks using highly sensitive pressure gauges. It is also a diagnostic tool to identify the locations of leaks. (Photo by John Curtis, © The Taunton Press, Inc.)

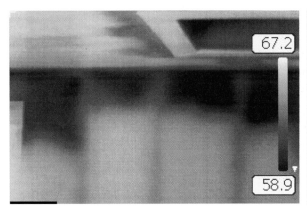

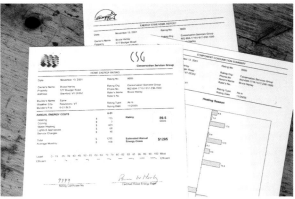

▲ An infrared scan shows missing wall insulation—this was taken indoors on a cold day. Blue areas show cold spots; yellow areas show warmer areas of good insulation. Note the slightly cooler studs (orange), the cold (uninsulated) attic hatch, and the areas around the hatch where insulation isn't working well. (Photo by Brett Monroe, Monroe Infrared Technologies.)

▲ A professional home performance analysis or home energy rating provides a thorough assessment of your home to help you plan a strategy and focus on the projects with the most benefit. (Photo © Kevin Kennefick.)

7 go green

HOME PERFORMANCE STARTS WITH ENERGY STAR

Look for Home Performance with ENERGY STAR® on the web and in your area. Home Performance with ENERGY STAR is a national model for addressing all your home energy and performance concerns in a unified package, using trained, qualified consultants and contractors. The Environmental Protection Agency sets the standards. Training, marketing support, and quality assurance is typically carried out at the state or utility sponsor level, and it includes some real financial support in some markets.

an air leakage test using a "blower door," and they should either probe your walls carefully or use an infrared camera to assess the insulation levels and quality.

They may test or carefully inspect your ducts for leaks. They should check your combustion equipment during the visit as well. Most will provide a detailed, computerized analysis of your whole home's energy performance.

8 GET HOME PERFORMANCE

There is a movement toward more comprehensive home energy assessments that include diagnostic testing, safety evaluations, and in-depth recommendations based on a performance evaluation of the whole house system.

Two national certification programs exist for professionals that you can trust: the Residential Energy Services Network (RESNET℠; www.resnet.us) certifies Home Energy Raters, and the Building Performance Institute (BPI; www.bpi.org) certifies Building Analysts. Both are excellent choices for getting a thorough home performance evaluation. You can also look for a certified Home Performance Analyst recognized by both organizations.

The EPA and U.S. Department of Energy jointly maintain a website that provides comprehensive information about all the ENERGY STAR programs (www.energystar.gov). See the "Home Improvement" and "Products" sections for the latest information and listings for your home energy needs.

▲ The Residential Energy Services Network (RESNET) and Building Performance Institute (BPI) provide professional certifications for Home Energy Raters and residential Building Analysts. These are the people you want when you need help.

9 GET HELP WITH THE WORK

Don't shy away from projects you can't do yourself because they may be beyond your skill or comfort level. These may be some of the biggest energy savers, and they are worth hiring a contractor who can do the job right.

Many chapters in this book suggest ways to identify qualified contractors for specific types of work. Of course, it's always a good idea to get multiple bids, but don't base your decision on price only. Talk to the contractors, find out how they work and what they pay attention to. Get referrals, and ask not only what went well, but how the contractor handled a situation when something went wrong.

10 GET FINANCIAL HELP

An increasing number of electric and gas utility companies and state agencies offer programs that provide some combination of technical support (audits and assessments), incentives or rebates, or access to attractive financing for energy improvements. Take advantage of all the assistance you can. For income-qualified homeowners, weatherization assistance is generally available through state or local community action agencies. Finally, there are a number of state and federal government tax credits that can help offset some of the cost. See Resources on p. 116 for more information.

11 PLAN AHEAD

As with any investment, energy efficiency improvements can benefit from a good plan. You probably won't do everything at once, but start by prioritizing. Plan on improvements that have a high cost/benefit ratio first, either because you get a lot of savings, or because implementing them is cheap. The savings can literally help you pay for more improvements. If you are inclined toward hands-on work, or want more in-depth information on insulation, heating and cooling systems, renovations, and ventilation systems, you may want to get my other book: *Insulate and Weatherize* (see Resources on p. 116).

Think about any equipment or appliances that are getting older—not only are older appliances less efficient, but the time to upgrade at a reasonable cost is when you are already paying to replace worn-out items. And consider plans to remodel or refinish rooms, or to replace exterior systems like siding or roofing. These can provide valuable opportunities to increase your home's efficiency at a modest additional cost.

12 go green

CONSIDER DOING MORE

Even as you focus on what's easily attainable and cost-effective, use the opportunity to do the best you possibly can with each project, large and small.

Whether fixing duct leaks and air leaks, adding insulation, replacing a heating or cooling system or your windows, or making a more substantial renovation, it's extremely unlikely you'll do this again for years to come.

If you plan to stay in the house indefinitely, even improvements that aren't cost-effective now will pay back faster as energy prices rise. And aggressive energy efficiency will help make your house inflation-resistant. If you don't stay in the house, these efforts will add value and reduce greenhouse gas emissions for years.

When choosing electronics and equipment, you'll see a theme repeated in this book: Don't settle for ENERGY STAR alone, but look beyond for the very highest efficiencies. Stretch as far as you can in every project you do—your planet, and your children, will thank you.

CHAPTER 2

Lighting and Plug-Ins

In this chapter and the next, we'll look at your electrical system and the many things in your home that run off it. Your electrical system doesn't "use" energy, it supplies energy to whatever devices are connected, ready, and waiting to be used.

Here we'll examine light fixtures, plug-in lamps, and many other common portable or semi-portable household items and review a variety of projects that can cut your electricity use. Most of these projects are inexpensive and require more thought and attention than time.

Monitor the Juice You Use

Although people sometimes suspect that their electric meters don't work properly, they almost always do. One of the toughest things for most of us to understand is how much energy the dozens of different electric devices in the home actually consume. Some run constantly, others see occasional use, and some use a lot of power, but only run intermittently. No matter what, the meter never stops turning.

How do you understand usage when your only feedback is one bill at the end of the month? An energy monitor can help you "see" what is happening in your house, so you can make better decisions about how you use electricity.

13 go green
CUT YOUR CARBON FOOTPRINT
Because electricity has two to three times the carbon emissions per unit of energy as fossil fuels, saving electric usage has a bigger effect on your greenhouse gas emissions than saving an equivalent amount of gas, oil, or propane. And because electricity costs more per unit of energy than fossil fuels, it also means more money back in your pocket.

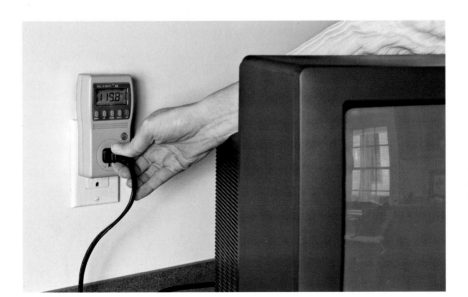

◀ An inexpensive energy monitor like this one ($30) can tell you how much any plug-in electrical device costs you, per hour or over a period of time. See Resources on p. 116 for suppliers.

14 energymyth

This is a myth born of laziness. The initial power surge from turning on any light, computer, or appliance consumes the same energy as just a few seconds of actual operation. So when you're not using it, turn it off.

15 TEST EACH APPLIANCE

One type of monitor works with plug-in lights and appliances—plug it into the wall, and plug the appliance into it. Following the directions, you can enter your electricity cost and find out how much each appliance costs to use. You can check each device individually to see how much it uses when it's on, and find out if it's really off when you turn it off.

You can also set it to monitor an item over time to find out how much that entertainment center or refrigerator uses in a week. This is especially useful for things like refrigerators or dehumidifiers that cycle on and off over time. This type of meter is less expensive than a whole-house meter and more convenient for checking one item at a time.

16 TEST YOUR WHOLE HOUSE

Another type of energy monitor checks your whole house at once. One product works by clamping onto your electric meter; another uses sensors installed in your main electrical panel (please follow directions carefully, and get help from an electrician if you need it).

The whole-house monitor checks all your electric users, including the lights and appliances that are wired directly to your house. It can tell you how many dollars per hour you use at any given time, as well as over time. Because they monitor the whole house at once, some of these meters have software to help you understand the use as individual items turn on and off (like your furnace fan). With others, it's up to you to turn items on and off to get a sense of how much electricity they use.

▶ A whole-house energy monitor is more expensive ($150 to $250), but it gives you feedback about the electrical use of your entire home, including permanently wired lights and appliances like furnace fans and pool pumps.

Seeing in the Dark

We need lights to read, work, and find our way to the bathroom in the middle of the night. We don't need to waste energy, and carbon emissions, with our lights. Lighting is sixth on the list of largest electricity consumers in the home (see the chart on p. 18), amounting to about $100 per year for the average household. It's also one of the easiest to cut—efficient lighting can shave 60 percent off that part of your bill.

17 INSTALL COMPACT FLUORESCENT LIGHTS

When I first started installing efficient compact fluorescent lights (CFLs) 18 years ago, they were disappointing. They took time to warm up, and they had a greenish tinge and awkward shapes that made them hard to install and harder to like. And they cost nearly $20 per bulb.

Now CFLs are smaller, are brighter, look better, and start instantly, and the price has come down to just a few dollars per bulb. Because they last eight to ten times longer than a regular bulb, they actually save you on replacement costs over several years—I still have CFLs in my kitchen that have been in use several hours a day for more than 14 years.

Install CFLs in any fixture that sees more than two hours of use at a time, such as lights in the kitchen, living/family room, and kids' rooms; outdoor lights; or any light on a daily timer. This gives you the most savings up front.

If you want to put CFLs in a light with a dimmer or electronic control, be sure to get one that is rated for a dimmer, otherwise it won't work properly and could be a fire hazard. This is also true for some electronic timer controls. Another thing to be careful about is that in very cold weather (well below freezing), some CFLs used in outdoor lights can start slowly or be dim for several minutes.

18 go green

INSTALL SOLAR ELECTRICITY

Solar electric panels, called photovoltaic (PV) modules, can be mounted on a roof or a stand to generate electricity to power your house and even run your meter backward when you generate more power than you use. PV panels reduce fossil fuel use and carbon emissions, but they are expensive. Even with state and federal tax credits and other grants, it's almost always more cost-effective to spend your money on energy efficiency first. Then, to be even more green, use your savings to pay for some solar panels.

◀ Solar-generated electricity using photovoltaic technology is a great way to reduce your electric bill and help the environment; however, it's almost always better to invest in efficiency first. (Photo by Christopher Derby-Kilfoyle, Berkshire Photovoltaic Services.)

Top 25 Electricity Users in American Homes

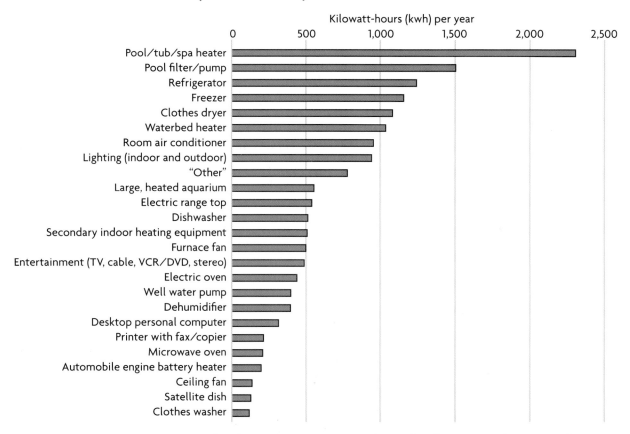

Kilowatt-hours (kwh) per year

Pool/tub/spa heater	
Pool filter/pump	
Refrigerator	
Freezer	
Clothes dryer	
Waterbed heater	
Room air conditioner	
Lighting (indoor and outdoor)	
"Other"	
Large, heated aquarium	
Electric range top	
Dishwasher	
Secondary indoor heating equipment	
Furnace fan	
Entertainment (TV, cable, VCR/DVD, stereo)	
Electric oven	
Well water pump	
Dehumidifier	
Desktop personal computer	
Printer with fax/copier	
Microwave oven	
Automobile engine battery heater	
Ceiling fan	
Satellite dish	
Clothes washer	

Note that these amounts represent averages for all users in each category. If you have any of these devices, your actual usage may be much higher or much lower than what's shown here. It also doesn't include usage for electric heating, central air-conditioning, or water heating.

▲ CFL floor lamps like this are much safer than units with halogen bulbs and use up to 80 percent less electricity than standard models. (Photo © Kevin Kennefick.)

▲ Using fixtures with built-in CFLs can save on replacement costs and energy, especially when you're planning to buy a light fixture anyway. Look for the ENERGY STAR label on the box. (Photo by Randy O'Rourke.)

▲ This CFL fixture has a special bulb that spreads the light around evenly behind the glass, getting more of it out where it's needed. (Photo by Randy O'Rourke.)

▲ Compact fluorescent lightbulbs use 60 percent to 70 percent less electricity, burn cooler, and last longer than regular lightbulbs. An ENERGY STAR label ensures efficiency and quality standards. (Photo by Scott Phillips, © The Taunton Press, Inc.)

19 REPLACE OLD LIGHT FIXTURES

Although many light fixtures accommodate the new, smaller CFLs, some types don't. In this case, or whenever you are buying a new light fixture, consider buying a pin-based CFL fixture.

Many lighting manufacturers have a range of good-quality light fixtures that utilize a plug-in (rather than screw-in) CFL bulb. There are two advantages: First, you don't have to buy the electronic base (called ballast) every time you replace the bulb, as you do with screw-in CFLs where the ballast is part of the bulb. Second, the fixtures are designed for CFLs, so many are more efficient at getting the light out of the fixture more effectively—giving you more light where you need it for each dollar of energy. This is especially true for CFL recessed "can" lights and exterior floodlights, where installing a screw-base CFL may reduce the available light.

◄ ▲ Good lighting in work areas allows you to use less overall lighting in your kitchen and other rooms. Under-cabinet lights make good task lights for countertops, and recessed halogen lights double as task lights for an island or table, offering accent lighting when used alone. Cove lights or recessed lights make good ambient lights. (Photos by Charles Bickford, courtesy *Fine Homebuilding*, © The Taunton Press, Inc.)

20 go green

PLEASE TURN OFF
THE LIGHTS

It's free, and it saves energy. From an early age, I was conditioned to turn the lights off whenever I leave a room. Doing that can save a lot of energy over time. Of course, when they *are* on, efficient lights are still better than regular lightbulbs. (Photo by Scott Phillips, © The Taunton Press, Inc.)

▲ For indoor or outdoor holiday light strings, LEDs can't be beat for both longevity and efficiency. (Photo by Randy O'Rourke.)

Total Annual Use Cost and Replacement Cost of Regular Bulbs Compared to CFLs

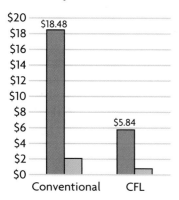

Based on 5 hours/day of usage, 75w bulb vs. 23w CFL.

22 energy myth

BECAUSE COMPACT FLUO-RESCENT LIGHTS CONTAIN MERCURY, THERE'S NO NET ENVIRONMENTAL BENEFIT

The tiny amount of mercury in CFLs is still a net gain for the environment. Coal-burning power plants are the largest man-made source of mercury in the environment, so the electricity saved over the life of one CFL actually reduces mercury emissions, as well as saving greenhouse gases and your money.

This prepaid shipping box can handle up to 12 CFLs for recycling, at less than $1.50 per bulb, from Energy Federation Incorporated (EFI). (Photo by Scott Phillips, © The Taunton Press, Inc.)

21 IMPROVE YOUR LIGHTING

Most of us want general area lighting mixed with focused task lighting. This is especially important in kitchens, where under-cabinet lights or pendant lights are more pleasing and more efficient than lighting the whole room with recessed can or ceiling fixtures. If you are planning a kitchen remodel, plan for maximum lighting efficiency.

Short strings of white holiday lights—used year-round—are a great way to add sparkle and background lighting without deep shadows, at only 20w to 40w. String them around windows, across beams, or around the edge of a ceiling (I have several strings in my house, on light switches so they are easy to turn on and off). LED (light-emitting diode) holiday lights use even less power.

LEDs, which are common in electronics, have been widely adopted for uses like traffic lights and exit signs, but they are not yet widely available as substitutes for regular lightbulbs. Although they do have some promise (they are super-efficient, are less bulky, and have a much longer life even than CFLs), they are still expensive, and those that are available have limited light output. Currently, the best LED products for homeowners are specialty applications: small spotlights for accent lighting, under-cabinet strip lights, candelabra/chandelier fixtures, and holiday light strings.

▲ Installing a new airtight, CFL-based insert is almost as easy as screwing in a new lightbulb. This dimmable unit from TCP costs about $40 (www.efi.org) and will help you save on your lighting bill, as well as your heating and cooling. (Photo by Randy O'Rourke.)

▲ The recessed-light insert has a built-in reflector that sits inside the existing recessed can. If the existing can is not tight to the drywall, you may need to caulk the gap before setting the insert in place. (Photo by Randy O'Rourke.)

23 INSTALL INSERTS FOR RECESSED LIGHTS

Recessed can lights have two problems: They have poor lighting efficiency and they leak air like crazy. First, identify priority fixtures that open into an attic or are mounted in cathedral ceilings. These may be replaced entirely with new, airtight cans that are rated for insulation contact. You may want the help of an electrician for that. You can then install CFL reflector bulbs that direct the light downward efficiently.

A simpler, less expensive solution is to fill each of these can lights with an insert that provides an air seal and a plug-in CFL bulb. The insert stops the airflow, and saves electric use. The CFL base means you don't have to buy replacement ballast with each bulb. Finally, for can lights in ceilings that have finished rooms above, simply replace the bulbs with screw-in CFL reflector bulbs.

▲ This compact fluorescent outdoor floodlight is a good choice if you want the light on for longer periods. (Photo by Randy O'Rourke.)

▲ A plug-in timer can ensure that you have light when you need it, and (unlike people) it won't forget to turn the lights off at bedtime. (Photo by Randy O'Rourke.)

▲ A screw-in daylight sensor will ensure that the light only comes on at night. (Photo by Scott Phillips, © The Taunton Press, Inc.)

▲ "Wall cube" power adapters use energy any time they are plugged in, even if nothing is attached. They are, however, getting smaller and more efficient over time. These cubes both charge the same cell phones, but the newer one (above) with the ENERGY STAR label uses a fraction of the power. (Photo by Randy O'Rourke.)

24 CONTROL YOUR LIGHTS

For outdoor security lights, or indoor lights used regularly, use a timer. For wired light fixtures, you'll need to install the timer in place of the on-off switch, so get the help of an electrician if you're not experienced with wiring projects.

For indoor plug-in lamps, buy a timer that plugs into the wall outlet. For exterior lights, here's an even better option: Install a motion-plus-daylight sensor. You don't even need to use CFL bulbs, because the lights will only be on for short periods (although a halogen floodlight will improve the efficiency of outdoor fixtures by about 30 percent). You can replace the whole fixture or add the sensors to an existing floodlight.

25 INSTALL A LIGHT TUBE

Also called a "tubular skylight," this is a great way to bring natural outdoor light into a dark area. A light tube also reduces the need for electric lights in dark areas. With a price tag of $200 to $500, it may take many years for the tube to pay for itself in saved electricity, but there are aesthetic and health benefits to natural light as well. It's cheaper than a skylight, is easier to install, and contributes less to winter heat loss and summer heat gain. Installation requires access to a roof or attic space directly above.

A light tube looks like a domed ceiling-light fixture, but instead of being powered by electricity, it's lit by natural sunlight from a collector dome on the roof.

▶ A tubular skylight provides natural outdoor light to dark spaces, without the carpentry or logistical hassles of installing a conventional skylight. (Photo by Krysta S. Doerfler, courtesy *Fine Homebuilding*, © The Taunton Press, Inc.)

▲ From inside the house, a light tube looks like a domed fixture, but it brings in bright natural light from outdoors and uses no electricity. (Photo by Krysta S. Doerfler, courtesy *Fine Homebuilding*, © The Taunton Press, Inc.)

26 go green

When it comes to standby power, not all electronics are the same. In a test comparing high-definition TVs, more than half of the 33 models in the 50-in. to 65-in. range used less than 1w in standby, with the lowest a 58-in. model that used 0.3w. Five in the 50-in. to 65-in. range used more than 20w continuously. The least efficient model was a 65-in. unit that consumed more than 76w when it's off —that's nearly $100 a year for just one TV. It used 250 times as much as the most efficient model and more than 27 times as much as the most efficient 65-in. unit. Standby power is not typically listed in the specs for consumer electronics, so you have to be a smart shopper. For HDTV test results, visit www.cnet.com and search for "television power consumption."

Plug Your Electricity Leaks

Besides lights, your home has lots of other plug-in electrical items. But when you turn off the switch, are they really off?

Many electronic gadgets use electricity whenever they're plugged in. Sometimes called "phantom loads" or "leaking electricity," these devices come in two types: those that maintain a "standby" state so you can turn them on with remote controls, to power clocks, or simply to wait for user input, like a printer; and those powered by plug-in "wall cubes" and AC/DC power supply adaptors. Both types typically use less power in standby mode than when fully on, but even so, it's equivalent to leaving a car idling 24/7 in your driveway, just so you don't have to bother cranking it on when it's time to go.

The VCR/DVD, cable box, network router—all can consume between 5w and 30w around the clock and may cost you $100 to $500 each year, amounting to roughly 5 percent of the average electricity bill. Cutting back on electrical use that has little or no tangible benefit saves you money and helps the environment.

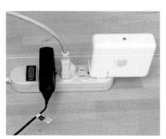

▲ Plug items that don't need to be on 24/7 into a power strip, and turn it off when you are finished.

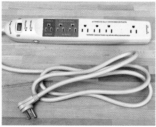

▲ This Smart Strip (www.efi.org) shuts off nonessential items (printer, scanner, monitor, VCRs, etc.) in a home office or entertainment center when you turn off the "main" item.

▲ Keep an eye on that entertainment center: Use a power strip or wall switch to turn off all the devices that don't have to stay on 24/7. (Photo by Andy Engel, courtesy *Fine Homebuilding*, © The Taunton Press, Inc.)

27 SWITCH IT OFF

tip Most families have several cell-phone chargers at home; unplug them when the phones aren't charging, or put them on a power strip.

Use a power strip for items that don't have to be on when you're not there, so you can really turn them off when you're not using them. Of course, some devices, like a digital video recorder or anything with a clock, need to be powered all the time.

Get a power strip with a lighted switch to help you remember when it's on. If you still have trouble remembering, a power strip that can help is the Smart Strip (see the center photo above). Also, if your house is wired with light-switch-controlled outlets, plug the nonessential items into those outlets. You can even replace the switch with a motion sensor; then the items turn on automatically when you enter the room.

28 TURN OFF THE SCREEN SAVER

If you use a desktop computer, this one choice can save you up to $100 a year. Screen savers were developed to prevent screens from burning out certain pixel areas during periods of inactivity. With today's technology, it's far better to "blank" the screen by turning the monitor off after a few minutes or put the whole computer in standby mode.

Many screen savers use complex graphics and actually increase computer power consumption. Some screen savers even prevent the power management software from operating, so it's best to completely deactivate all screen savers.

29 GIVE YOUR COMPUTER A REST

Lull your computer to sleep—use "standby" or "hibernate" mode. If you have Microsoft® Windows®, go to "Control Panel—Power Options." Choose the power scheme "max energy savings" (or "max battery" for laptops). Or, you can set custom time delays for inactivity until the system shuts off the monitor or hard drive, or goes into standby.

On a Mac®, choose "System Preferences—Energy Saver"; it's called "sleep" instead of standby. You can independently set times for the monitor or the computer to go to sleep. On either system, when the monitor is off, the computer keeps working in the background. In standby or sleep, activity stops, but it takes just a few seconds to turn back on, right where you left off. Any machine can easily be configured to wake up automatically for scheduled events, or when a fax or modem rings.

◄ In Windows, the "Power Options" setting allows independent settings for screen, hard drive, standby, and hibernate modes. Additional tabs allow customizing power mode buttons ("Advanced") and enabling of a no-power "Hibernate" mode.

30 BE AN ENERGY STAR SHOPPER

One of the best ways to help reduce energy use is to buy products with an ENERGY STAR label whenever you can. ENERGY STAR has labels for efficient home electronics in the following categories: battery chargers for cordless tools, appliances, and personal care products; power adapters; cordless phones; digital-to-analog converter boxes; home audio components; DVD products; and TVs and VCR.

With the popularity of home offices, it's worth knowing about ENERGY STAR–rated office equipment as well. These product groups include computers, notebook computers, tablet PCs, and computer monitors; printers, scanners, and all-in-ones; copier and fax machines; digital duplicators; mailing machines; and water coolers.

31 energy myth

TURNING YOUR COMPUTER OFF WEARS IT OUT, SO IT'S BETTER TO LEAVE IT ON

This is a holdover from 1980s technology, when hard drives were prone to failure. Modern computers don't suffer from power cycling. In fact, turning them off or putting them in standby helps them last longer by reducing heat and mechanical wear. With modern energy-saving technologies, and much more stable operating systems, using a standby, sleep, or hibernate mode will get you back up and running reliably, much faster than rebooting.

tip On a desktop computer, don't shut off the machine with a power strip if it's in standby, because you can lose your work. Hibernate (available with Windows) is an advanced standby mode that saves the computer's entire operating state to the hard drive. This allows you to cut power completely to your computer; when a laptop hibernates, it literally shuts off the battery. When you turn a computer back on from hibernate, it comes up right where you left off. Hibernate is the best type of standby mode for long periods, especially overnight, because you can safely turn the power off completely.

CHAPTER 3

Big Appliances

 Appliances are the biggest electricity hogs in your house. Pool and spa heaters and pumps, refrigerators and freezers, dryers, and room air conditioners top the list in the average home (see the chart on p.18).

The appliances I cover in this chapter account for nearly 40 percent of all home electricity use nationwide, so strategies to make them more efficient can bring big rewards—for your comfort, your bank account, and the environment.

We'll cover two basic approaches to these big energy users: first, making sure that when you replace one of these larger items, you buy the most efficient model available that meets your needs; second, getting the best efficiency out of your existing appliances.

Let's Get Efficient

In most cases, replacing an appliance with a new, more efficient model won't save you enough to pay for the new appliance—at least not in any reasonable amount of time. But when you retire an older unit, upgrading to a high-efficiency replacement is a great investment.

The time to do some research is when you start to think about a replacement. Depending on the appliance, it really doesn't pay to wait until it breaks down—an urgent replacement will hardly allow you the time to shop around for the most efficient model.

tip Getting to know the capabilities and weak points of home electronics and appliances should start with a visit to the U.S. Department of Energy's Energy Efficiency and Renewable Energy website (www.eere.energy.gov/consumer) and ENERGY STAR (www.energystar.gov). Here, you can find key information about shopping for efficient appliances, read up on energy standards for residential appliances, and learn how to estimate the amount of energy the appliances in your own house will use.

▶ Look for appliances with the lowest estimated operating cost; in other words, look for the EnergyGuide sticker with the arrow as close to the left side of the scale as possible. The sticker for this dishwasher shows that it is so efficient it's actually off the scale. Also note the ENERGY STAR label printed on the bottom right hand corner.

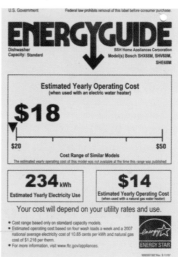

25

33 USE ENERGY STAR

The U.S. government's ENERGY STAR labeling program includes categories for refrigerators and freezers, dehumidifiers, clothes washers, and room air conditioners. The ENERGY STAR label identifies the top tier of efficiency for each category, but with some appliances, you can often do better even within the range of ENERGY STAR products.

All of these appliances (except dehumidifiers) are also required to display a yellow "EnergyGuide" label, regardless of their efficiency level. The label is not the same as an ENERGY STAR rating; the most efficient and least efficient appliances have this label, as does everything in between. And definitely look for electric utility rebates or other programs that can help you with the cost of the upgrade. Also check out www.aceee.org/consumerguide, a regularly updated, independent, high-quality information resource focused on high levels of efficiency.

34 UPGRADE YOUR REFRIGERATOR

In most cases, the refrigerator is the single largest electricity user in your home, typically exceeded only by a pool, a spa, an electric water heater, or electric heat. Refrigerators have improved a lot in recent years. Today's ENERGY STAR models use half the electricity of government minimum standards before 1993. But be aware that, for refrigerators and freezers, both the ENERGY STAR and EnergyGuide labels only compare units of similar size and features. Models with features that reduce energy efficiency, like side-by-side and through-door services, are only compared with similar models.

Use the estimated energy use of the unit (shown in dollars and kwh per year on the EnergyGuide label) to compare models. For example, a 20-cu.-ft. top freezer without ice maker that meets ENERGY STAR requirements uses 432kwh/year; a 26-cu.-ft. side-by-side ENERGY STAR unit with ice may use as much as 600 kwh—almost 50 percent more. And although the ENERGY STAR label requires 15 percent less energy use than current minimum standards, there are some units that actually save 20 percent to 50 percent.

▶ Although side-by-side doors and through-door ice and water units are not the most efficient options, this model by Maytag meets ENERGY STAR requirements for its size and type. It also warns you when the door is left ajar, and it automatically limits energy-wasting defrost cycles when it isn't opened for several days. (Photo courtesy Maytag Corp.)

When shopping for a new refrigerator, avoid energy-wasting features such as through-door ice and water dispensers, even if it means a little less convenience, and look for a model with an open-door alarm. A model with a top freezer uses 10 percent to 15 percent less energy than a side-by-side. A bottom freezer with a pull-out drawer compartment does almost as well, and it may rival or even beat the side-by-side for convenience. And if you're in the market for a freezer, consider a manual-defrost freezer. I bought a chest-type commercial freezer with an ENERGY STAR label; after more than three years, it still has barely any frost at all.

35 MONITOR THE TEMPERATURE

A little care can help keep your fridge running as efficiently as it can. Buy a small fridge thermometer, and adjust the thermostat so it maintains 38°F to 42°F. Adjust the freezer to stay between 0°F and 5°F. Turn the switch to the "economy" or "power saving" setting, if that's an option, and switch off the condensation control. You may need to set it to "normal" at times in humid weather, but don't forget to set it back.

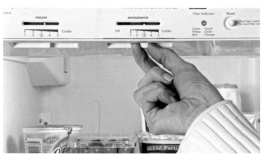

◄ Most refrigerators don't show the actual temperature settings, so adjust the thermostat based on your thermometer readings. Look at the thermometer after the refrigerator has been unopened for an hour or more.

36 go green

When you buy a new fridge or freezer, don't keep the old one running in the garage or basement. It's just as inefficient as ever. If you really need more capacity, buy another small one that's as efficient as you can find. Or, if you really need extra refrigeration once in a while (for example, during holidays), leave the second fridge unplugged for the 46 weeks a year you don't really need it. Be responsible about disposal, as well: If your local utility company doesn't have a program for disposing of the old junker, find out about recycling programs for refrigerant-containing appliances (www.aceee.org/consumerguide/disposal.htm).

◄ A simple refrigerator thermometer allows you to monitor the temperature in your fridge—the ideal setting is between 38°F and 42°F. The freezer should be between 0°F and 5°F.

tip Manual defrost (or partially automatic defrost) refrigerators and freezers are significantly more efficient than automatic units—but you do have to defrost them regularly to maintain their efficiency. Ice buildup acts as an insulator and makes the compressor work harder to keep food cold.

Spend a few minutes every other month cleaning the coils, and periodically check the door seals to make sure they are tight. And try to make sure that the fridge can get rid of heat effectively—a refrigerator should not be enclosed in a cabinet or box, or placed too close to a heat source (like an oven).

One last thing: Don't worry too much about standing with the door open. Unless the fridge is nearly empty, it doesn't make as much difference as most people think.

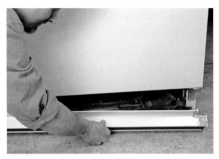

▲ It's not a fun job, but you should clean the coils under your refrigerator at least every two months (more often if you have pets). Be sure to follow the directions in the owner's manual before starting this job, including unplugging the fridge if recommended.

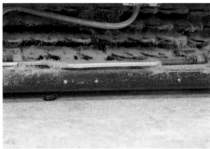

▲ The refrigerant coils are designed to give off heat to the room, and dust and pet hair act as insulation and cut airflow.

▲ Don't jam the vacuum cleaner wand between the coils, because it could damage them. This coil brush ($2.95 at www.efi.org) is designed to sweep dirt out of the coils from behind, so you can safely bring the dirt to the vacuum.

38 GET A FRONT-LOADING WASHER

When I was in college, I always used the big front-loading washer at the coin-op laundry. Not only could I wash a huge load for only a couple of extra quarters, but it was easier on my clothes and it spun them really well, which saved me quarters later at the dryer.

Home versions of these front-loading machines have been on the market for years and use much less electricity and water than standard machines. They operate with a back-and-forth "sloshing" action of the horizontal drum, using gravity rather than a brute-force "agitator" to keep things moving. They wash effectively with less soap, and they spin the water out much faster with far less vibration. (You do have to watch them, because if they can't balance the load for spinning, they will just cancel the cycle, and you'll have to rearrange and spin again.)

Another benefit to buying a new front-loading washer: New top-loading washers have made design compromises to keep up with increasing federal efficiency standards, and many new models just don't work as well.

39 go green

Use cold water in the washer as much as possible, with soaps that are suited to cold washing. It'll use less energy and costs you nothing. (Note: Front-loading washers need less soap than older models.) If your washer has the option, it is a good idea to use the temperature-regulated "warm" cycle for washing rather than "hot." It'll use less hot water than an equal mix of hot and cold. And remember not to overload or underload the machine, which will reduce efficiency. Pay attention to recommendations for load size in the user manual for wash effectiveness.

▲ Front-loading clothes washers are not only more energy efficient but fit nicely into a compact area. You can install a counter above a washer-dryer pair for convenient folding, or stack them up and down. (Photo courtesy GE/Power Creative.)

40 go green

The most efficient option for drying clothes is hanging them outside or on racks to dry. It uses no energy at all, although it takes a few minutes. For the best of both worlds, machine-dry clothes for 10 to 15 minutes, just enough to fluff them up and get the lint out. Then hang them until completely dry, saving energy and leaving them smelling fresher than any fabric softener can.

A clothesline is a traditional technology that provides the highest level of energy efficiency. In my house, a couple of wooden drying racks do the job when the weather doesn't cooperate. (photo by Michael Jastremski for openphoto.net.)

41 DRY SMART

You can't really buy an "officially" efficient clothes dryer, because dryers have no EnergyGuide label or efficiency rating. Dryers use heat from electricity or natural gas to dry clothes, and there is not much room for improving efficiency.

The largest efficiency gain in drying clothes comes from an efficient clothes washer—spinning more water out reduces the need for drying by half or more. What you can do is avoid running the dryer longer than you need to, so don't use a timed cycle. Newer dryers use moisture sensors—you can set them to stop as soon as the clothes are ready, so less energy is wasted.

The best-quality and most effective moisture sensors are right in the dryer drum, but any moisture sensor will help prevent wasted drying at the end of the cycle.

42 GIVE YOUR DRYER AN OVERHAUL

Dryers depend on airflow, so the most important regular maintenance you can perform is to keep the exhaust duct clean.

Make sure you clean the lint filter every time you use the dryer, too, and if the filter doesn't fit tightly, replace it so lint doesn't go around it, clogging up the vent and possibly creating a fire hazard. If you have a ribbed vinyl dryer hose, replace it with a smooth metal one that won't clog up with lint.

▶ Never vent a dryer into your basement (or anywhere else inside the house); to also run a dehumidifier right next to it is about the most expensive way possible to dry your clothes. (Photo by Bruce Harley, © Conservation Services Group.)

43 USE YOUR DISHWASHER SMARTLY

If you wait until it's full, the dishwasher can use 30 percent less water than washing dishes by hand, but don't run a partial load, because that wastes hot water.

Choose the "energy saver" or equivalent setting for everyday use, and avoid high-heat cycles for everyday use. Turn off the automatic drying cycle, avoid prerinsing dishes, and, if you're not going to fill up the dishwasher, use the rinse-and-hold cycle.

Modern dishwashers are more effective at removing food, and the best ones sense particulate in the water so they "know" exactly when to stop. When you do need to replace the dishwasher, buy an ENERGY STAR model, and look for units with soil sensors and a no-heat drying option. Some innovative energy-saving features to look for include steam-cycle models, drawer-mounted units, and "condensation" drying.

45 go green

When you hand-wash dishes, don't run the hot water. Use a dishpan or fill the sink to create a bath for washing or rinsing dishes. And turn the water on and off when you need it with an aerator that has a flip lever (see p. 43).

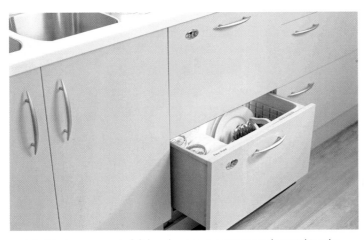

▲ A double drawer-mounted dishwasher can save you energy by matching the load size to the dishes: If you only fill one drawer, you run only a small load at full capacity. (Photo courtesy Fisher & Paykel Appliances.)

▲ Many dishwashers have an "energy saver" cycle; this dishwasher by Bosch® has an EcoOption™ button that cuts wash water temperature while extending the wash cycle. Photo courtesy Bosch Appliances.)

44 COOK ENERGY SMART

There isn't much you can do about the efficiency of an oven or range top, other than being a smart user. First, use a microwave or toaster oven for small meals or reheating, because they use much less power than a regular oven or stove top. And don't open the oven door to check on food if you can avoid it. Trust the timer, or use the oven light and window.

When cooking on the range, match the burner size to the pot to avoid waste. Finally, keep gas ovens clean and tuned up to prevent deadly carbon monoxide (CO). Don't pile pans or foil at the bottom next to the burner. If you get a home performance professional to do an energy assessment, ask about testing oven CO levels for safety.

There are no ENERGY STAR ratings for ovens or ranges, but when you buy a new range or oven, consider a convection oven—the internal fan cuts cooking time. If replacing an electric range or cooktop, choose one with induction-type burners; these are significantly more efficient than a standard or radiant stove.

▲ Using a flame or electric burner that's larger than the pot may seem to do the job faster, but it really doesn't, and it also wastes heat.

Air-Conditioning

46 energymyth

AN AIR CONDITIONER THAT RUNS CONTINUOUSLY USES MORE ENERGY

Actually, a smaller air conditioner, with a smaller compressor and fan, running for an hour uses less energy than a larger one running for 20 or 30 minutes at a time. And if you live in a humid climate, longer run times provide more effective dehumidification.

Air conditioners and dehumidifiers are refrigerant-based appliances that can keep you comfortable and can consume a lot of energy in the process.

Here, we'll discuss ways to ensure your equipment is running at top efficiency, as well as purchasing tips to use when you're in the market for a new one. We'll cover central air-conditioning in chapter 5.

47 KEEP WINDOW UNITS RUNNING WELL

Room air conditioners are seventh on the list of electricity-consuming appliances in homes (see the chart on p. 18), so it's important to keep them tuned up. First of all, free airflow is essential: Always install air conditioners so that the indoor and outdoor surfaces are unobstructed. The first time I ever installed a room air conditioner, it was in an attic apartment with deep interior window wells. Balancing most of the unit's weight outdoors made me nervous, so I figured I'd take advantage of the shelf and install most of the unit inside, with only the back exposed outdoors. Unfortunately, that left more than half the exterior air vents indoors—and I wondered why the room didn't cool off.

Also, be sure to use stick-on foam weatherstripping to seal gaps around the window sash and to keep the cool air in and the warm air out. Other important maintenance tasks include changing or cleaning the interior air filter regularly and keeping the exterior clean and free of debris.

Finally, don't let your air conditioner turn into a heat-loss machine when you aren't using it: Remove it in the winter. At the very least, use a sealed, insulating cover. Chapter 5 has additional tips for making air-conditioning more efficient by reducing the need for cooling in your home in the first place.

▶ Don't install a window or through-wall air conditioner in a restricted space; if the air can't circulate properly, the air conditioner will work twice as hard to keep you cool.

▲ The ENERGY STAR label on this dehumidifier tells you that it's efficient—but you have to clean it regularly to keep it running right.

◄ Clean or replace your air conditioner filter regularly during the cooling season to ensure good indoor airflow. Be careful to re-install it properly to prevent air getting past the filter. (Photo by John Curtis, © The Taunton Press, Inc.)

48 BUY THE RIGHT SIZE ENERGY STAR AIR CONDITIONER

With air conditioners, bigger is not better. Efficiency is much worse during the first few minutes of operation, so an oversize unit that starts and stops more often spends more time in the low-efficiency "startup" mode. If it's the right size, the unit should run almost continuously on a hot day to provide maximum efficiency.

Although most people (and manufacturers) base sizing on room area, that really doesn't work; www.cooloff.org provides an online worksheet for properly figuring the size of a room air conditioner based on the number and type of windows and insulation levels in the house. Also important, look for a unit with the highest Energy Efficiency Rating (EER); ENERGY STAR units range from 10 percent to 36 percent better than federal minimum standards, so use the ENERGY STAR label as a minimum. Go to aceee.org/consumerguide/cooling.htm or download the air conditioner list from the ENERGY STAR website for more detailed information about the highest-efficiency units available.

49 IMPROVE YOUR DEHUMIDIFIER EFFICIENCY

If you need to use a dehumidifier regularly, try to reduce moisture in your home and basement first (see the "Tip" on p. 101). Also, vent your dryer correctly (see p. 30) and ensure that your air conditioner is running properly (see pp. 58–64).

If you attach a hose to drain the water automatically, make sure the water doesn't end up back inside—I've seen dehumidifiers with hoses leading to backed-up floor drains that are trying to dry out the water sitting in the backed-up drain—obviously working very hard to push water nowhere.

Make sure that air can flow easily around the unit, and carefully follow the manufacturer's instructions for cleaning. Of course, buy an ENERGY STAR–labeled product when it's time to purchase a dehumidifier. Like other appliances, look at the product specifications. Even ENERGY STAR–labeled units have a range of energy factors from 1.2 liters to more than 3 liters per kwh (higher is better).

Fresh Air Ventilation

Most people think of ventilation in the home as the bathroom fan, and maybe a kitchen exhaust. I once asked a group of high school students about their impression of the typical bathroom fan, and they agreed on two things right away: These fans are noisy, and they generally don't work. They are rarely used, because they don't do much. We need effective ventilation systems in homes, and windows alone aren't adequate, because most of us don't like to open windows when it's very cold or hot outside.

50 INSTALL MECHANICAL VENTILATION

Mechanical ventilation systems typically maintain a continuous low flow of exhaust or supply air and effectively remove moisture and pollutants from the kitchen and bathroom. They don't have to cost a lot; in the simplest type of system, you can replace a standard bathroom fan with a high-quality ENERGY STAR–labeled unit that is designed for continuous low speed and quiet operation. Some models also provide a high-speed boost when you're in the bathroom.

▶ This efficient bathroom fan uses only 23w, and it's so quiet you won't even know it's running. It also has a built-in compact fluorescent light fixture. Some models have built-in, low-speed operation that uses even less electricity.

▲ Look for a bathroom fan that is quiet, is long lasting, and uses very low power. (Photo courtesy Panasonic.)

◀ A wind-up timer connected to the fan is one way to ensure the fan runs long enough to get the moisture out and also shuts off after you leave the bathroom.

It's important that the fan exhaust leads to the outdoors through a short, smooth metal duct that doesn't choke the air (in most climates, if the duct runs through the attic, it must be insulated to prevent condensation). Combined with a simple timer to control fresh-air cycles, these systems help ensure that a minimum amount of fresh air is drawn into the home and bathroom moisture is removed effectively. There are other types of central ventilation systems; see Resources on p. 116 for more information.

tip Avoid "room air cleaners," ozone generators, ion generators, and any other gizmos that claim to solve air quality problems just by plugging them in. Typically, they don't help, and some can actually create pollutants in your home, consuming electricity all the while.

◀ Kitchen range hoods, when installed and vented properly, effectively draw grease, moisture, and heat up and away. (Photo courtesy Viking.)

▲ The fan-delay timer, at left, turns the fan and light on at the same time. But when you turn off the light, the fan continues to run for a preset time to allow adequate removal of moisture. Or, use a wind-up timer, at right; it guarantees you'll never forget to turn the fan off. (Photo © Kevin Kennefick.)

▲ Automatic timers can control a continuously operating fan as a low-cost fresh-air ventilation system. The Airetrak™ (left) can run the fan at a low speed for 5 to 60 minutes every hour; when you press the button, it runs the fan at full speed for 20 minutes. A 24-hour pin timer (center) can operate the fan on any schedule you choose. Controls are available for $30 to $90 (www.efi.org/store). (Photo © Kevin Kennefick.)

▲ Energy-recovery ventilation systems like this one provide both dedicated fresh air and exhaust. They use the exhaust air to preheat (or precool) incoming fresh air. I recommend these systems in very tight, efficient homes, or for homeowners who have special needs when it comes to indoor air quality. (Photo courtesy Venmar.)

51 RUN YOUR CEILING FANS EFFICIENTLY

tip — Be wary of "temperature-controlled" settings on ceiling fans—they may actually waste energy. If the fan is controlled by a thermostat and comes on whenever the temperature warms up, it will run even when nobody is in the room—generating more heat and cooling no one.

Ceiling fans can keep you cool, but only when you're in the room. Otherwise, they just generate heat while they run, so shut them off when you leave. One option is to install a motion sensor, so the fan shuts off automatically. But be careful: Some models with remote controls may not work properly with a motion sensor, so read the manufacturer's instructions first.

The best option is to replace your ceiling fans with ENERGY STAR models. ENERGY STAR ceiling fans use less than half the electricity of standard fans, and they run more quietly. As with other appliances, there is a wide range of efficiency within the available ENERGY STAR products—download the list from the ENERGY STAR website to find the detailed efficiency ratings.

▶ This high-efficiency ceiling fan by Hampton Bay® moves nearly 50% more air per unit of energy than models that just meet ENERGY STAR standards, and more than twice as much as a typical ceiling fan. This one also has an efficient light built in, and comes with remote controls. (Photo © Terri Glanger Photography.)

Energy-Wasting Water

A few other energy users are worth mentioning because they can cost you a great deal of electrical energy and hundreds of dollars each year to operate. They all involve water—for large aquariums, for swimming pools, and for hot tubs and spas.

52 THE HIDDEN COST OF FISH

A heated aquarium can be a significant electricity user; in fact, it's number 10 on the list of electricity-guzzling home appliances. The amount of energy used by an aquarium varies a lot, but most of it is used by heaters that control the tank temperature.

On the high end, this water heating may cost upward of $300 a year. But two things can reduce that energy use: Set the tank temperature lower, or set the room temperature higher, especially in air-conditioning season. Keeping an aquarium at 78°F in a room that is 65°F requires two to three times as much energy as in a room that is 75°F. Also, using a smaller tank can help. A 55-gal. tank uses two to three times as much energy as a 22-gal. tank.

One more option is to choose fish species that don't require such a warm tank. Information on "cool water" (unheated) aquarium setup and fish species is readily available online or in bookstores.

53 go green

Using electricity is the least efficient (and most expensive) way to heat water, whether it's your potable hot water supply, your fish tank, or a hot tub. For most of the country, it means burning coal or other fuels at a power plant to heat water that runs a turbine at 35 percent efficiency; if you can burn the fuel at home to heat water, the efficiency is more like 80 percent! Of course, it's not practical for many appliances that need localized hot water; for example, the approach for booster heaters in dishwashers is to reduce the amount of water that needs heating, rather than include a separate gas boiler in the unit. The most efficient way to heat water is to eliminate or reduce the need for hot water: for example, use a cold-water fish so you don't have to heat the water at all.

◄ Heating an aquarium can cost far more than the price of the fish—$100 to $300 a year. Heaters are optional, however, with many fish species.

54 COVER YOUR POOL OR SPA

Pool and spa heaters are the biggest users—that's number one—on the list of energy-hungry appliances (see p. 18).

If you have a heated pool, the biggest source of heat loss is the open top, so installing a sliding or rolling cover, and using it, can save a bundle. Another option to consider is a solar pool heater. It requires professional installation, but solar pool heating is a well-developed technology that can handle most or all seasonal pool-heating needs.

If you have a spa, make sure to get an insulating cover and keep it on whenever you aren't using the spa. Evaporation is as detrimental as direct heat loss, so be sure the cover provides a snug seal all the way around—and don't be fooled by cheap floating covers.

An outdoor spa should be completely filled underneath with closed-cell foam insulation, or else the base should be insulated around its perimeter with at least 3 in. of foam. If you have a spa and it doesn't have the appropriate levels of insulation, you can add more, either by spraying foam against the bottom of the tub itself or by adding rigid polystyrene foam around the perimeter of the cabinet.

And don't be fooled by the claims of "reflective" foil-faced bubble-type insulation—the performance is disappointing (see the "Tip" on p. 93). Stick with conventional sprayed or rigid foam insulation.

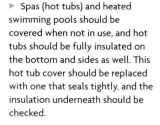

▶ Spas (hot tubs) and heated swimming pools should be covered when not in use, and hot tubs should be fully insulated on the bottom and sides as well. This hot tub cover should be replaced with one that seals tightly, and the insulation underneath should be checked.

55 CONTROL YOUR POOL PUMP

Even an unheated pool has a circulation/filtration pump, and almost all swimming pool pumps are bigger than they need to be, which can waste several hundred dollars a year.

Pool pumping is the second-largest electric appliance use, and I offer three basic approaches to saving pump energy:

The first is a modest project, but it can still save 60 percent of your pool pump costs. Install a timer on the pump so it doesn't run full time (or hire an electrician to do so). If you're lucky enough to have a timer already, adjust it so that it runs for shorter periods.

The purpose of the pump is to filter pool water and mix the chemicals, but longer run times don't always mean better performance. In fact, many pool owners are happy with pumping only three to six hours per day. Start by setting the timer to run six hours each day (two-hour runs spaced evenly around the clock). If the pool stays clear, try cutting the run time further. If the pool becomes cloudy, increase the run time by one-half hour per day until you are satisfied.

56 MAINTAIN YOUR POOL

To minimize the time you need to run a pool pump, it's important to keep it working effectively. Monitor the water filter, and change it when needed based on the manufacturer's recommendations. A proper installation should include a pressure gauge on each side of the filter, so you know when it needs replacement; as the filter clogs up, the difference in pressure during pump operation will increase. A pool cover will also reduce the amount of debris getting into the pool, saving your filters and further reducing run time.

57 INSTALL A SMALLER POOL PUMP

Most residential pool pumps are 1.5 hp; half of that (.75 hp) is usually adequate. The most efficient choice is a low-speed pump (1,725 rpm instead of 3,450 rpm), or a two-speed pump running on low speed for circulation (the higher speed may be needed to operate a pool sweep or solar pool heater, or during peak use).

Changing the pump is a professional job; if your existing pump works, it's probably not worth the cost to replace the pump just to save energy, unless you live in a warm climate and operate the pool most of the year. But when your pump needs service or replacement, that's the time to look into downsizing. Proper sizing of the pump depends on the piping configuration. Based on the pool installation, it may also help to reconfigure some of the piping. Larger diameter pipes, replacement of sharp 90° elbows with two 45° elbows (or flexible connectors), and an oversize filter (rated at least 50 percent higher than the design flow rate) all reduce the pressure seen by the pump and increase the flow, reducing the energy required (see Resources on p. 116 for more information).

Note that with a smaller pump, especially a low-speed pump, you may have to increase the run time again. But running a smaller motor more hours is still a big energy saver overall.

▶ You can control the circulating pump on your swimming pool with a timer like this one that allows it to run part time each day, preferably for several short periods spread out over the day. Cut back on the daily run time until you notice the water quality begin to degrade, then increase it a bit.

CHAPTER 4

Hot Water

 When it comes to hot water, we waste energy three ways: unnecessary use, like an inefficient showerhead; pipes or faucets that leak or drip; or heat escaping from the hot water system, up the chimney or out from pipes.

Using Less

Using less hot water quite simply leads to paying less for the energy used to heat it. In this chapter, we focus on sinks and showers. (I've covered dishwashers and clothes washers in chapter 3.)

Most of the projects I'll be walking you through in this chapter are projects you can do yourself. In other words, where you might need a contractor of some type—such as an HVAC contractor or a plumber or a carpenter—to do some of the energy fixes I get into in other parts of this book, here you can accomplish some energy savings—and resulting cost savings—without a lot of help.

For these projects, gather a pair of channel-lock pliers, a large adjustable wrench, a couple of thick rags, plumber's Teflon® tape, and the new devices you want to install. It may help to have a piece of rubber several inches square, like a kitchen jar-lid opener or a piece of a bicycle tire inner tube to protect metal finishes from the wrench and pliers.

tip Electricity is an expensive fuel for water heating, but if you don't already have a gas line, it is likely your only option. If you live in a warm or hot climate, consider a *heat pump water heater* for high efficiency. It actually uses heat from your home or basement to make hot water, and it produces some cooling at the same time. This emerging technology is not yet available "off the shelf" from plumbing and heating contractors; manufacturers are listed in Resources (see p. 116).

◄ No matter its style or size, a bathroom is at its best when sinks don't leak and showerheads make the most of water flow. (Photo by Brian Pontolilo, courtesy *Fine Homebuilding,* © The Taunton Press.)

58 INSTALL A LOW-FLOW AERATOR

To use less hot water without compromising convenience, install a low-flow faucet aerator. The aerator is the screw-in insert right at the outlet of the faucet. If an aerator already has a stamp showing a rating of 1.0 gpm (gallons per minute) or less, you can skip this step. For those that don't, buy 1.0 gpm aerators, which should fit your faucet (most have a standard screw-thread size).

Here are the steps:

1 Unscrew the old aerator. You may need channel-lock pliers if it's very tight.

2 Screw in the replacement. Hand-tightening is usually enough, but if it leaks around the sides, you may have to use pliers—wrap a heavy rag or small piece of rubber around the sides so you don't mar the finish.

▶ Once the old aerator is removed, the new one (left) screws easily into place.

▶ This new faucet aerator uses 1.0 gpm; the old one used 1.5 gpm. Many older aerators are unrated and use 2.0 gpm to 3.0 gpm.

59 CONTROL THE FLOW

An aerator with an on/off button or lever is especially helpful in a kitchen sink for washing dishes or even getting a cup of water. The lever stops the water just as it leaves the faucet (allowing a small dribble to remind you that the faucet is still on). You can "switch" the water on and off with one finger, while keeping the temperature and flow you like.

These aerators are also helpful in the bathroom for tasks like shaving, which require intermittent hot water. Install these exactly like a standard aerator; try to get the lever pointed in a convenient direction. Many levers are reversible, so you don't have to overtighten it to get the lever around to the front.

tip Wash dishes smartly. It's good to use a lever-type aerator when you wash dishes by hand; use a tub or wash sink with soapy water, and only use the faucet intermittently for rinsing. Unless you're a fanatic, though, it generally uses significantly less hot water to run the dishwasher.

◄ The lever on this kitchen sink aerator is especially useful on a two-handle faucet: Turn the flow on and off while the water temperature remains constant. (Photo by John Curtis.)

60 energy myth

A TIMER ON AN ELECTRIC WATER HEATER WILL SAVE ENERGY

A timer actually won't save heat, unless you have a very badly insulated water heater, and it won't save you money unless you have a time-of-use utility rate. What *will* save you energy is to turn the tank off at the circuit breaker any time you leave the house for more than a couple of days. (If you have a gas water heater, set it to "vacation" or "pilot.") Just remember that it will take a little while to heat up when you get home.

61 REPLACE SHOWERHEADS

Some older low-flow showerheads used 2.5 gpm and provided a very unsatisfying shower. Today, you can buy standard or massage-type low-flow models that are designed to provide excellent showers, using as little as 1.5 gpm.

If the shower arm comes loose while removing the old showerhead, replace it; these are available at any hardware store or home center. Just wrap the threads with Teflon tape before threading it into the fitting inside the wall, and be careful not to pull sideways on the arm as you're tightening.

Here's how to replace the showerhead:

▲ Don't do this on a Sunday evening; if the shower arm breaks off, you may get stuck.

1 Unscrew the old showerhead using channel-lock pliers (or an adjustable wrench, if the old nut has flat sides). Be gentle.

2 Wrap the threads of the shower arm clockwise with a few turns of Teflon tape.

3 Screw in the new showerhead, and tighten it gently with the channel-lock pliers (protecting the finish with rubber or a rag) or an adjustable wrench. Push on the wrench in the direction of the wall, not parallel to the wall, so you don't stress the shower arm where it threads into a fitting inside the wall.

4 Test it to be sure there are no leaks.

▲ Wrap several turns of plumber's tape tightly clockwise around the threads to ensure no leaks. The tape is not sticky, so lightly mold it into the threads as you turn.

▲ If the new showerhead has two flat sides, tighten it with an adjustable wrench.

▲ This showerhead gives an amazingly satisfying shower at only 1.5 gpm—just over half the standard 2.5 gpm rate.

62 LOWER THE TEMPERATURE

Both gas and electric water heaters are adjustable. You will save money if you set the heater at the lowest setting you can get by with—just don't go below 120°F.

Note, though, that not all gas water heaters have a thermostat that turns "up" in the same direction, so look at the markings on the knob. If you have an electric water heater, start by turning off the circuit breaker. Electric water heaters have two thermostats; access them by removing the two metal covers (sometimes both are under one long cover) with a screwdriver.

Using the screwdriver, set both at the same temperature. After adjusting, check the temperature several times over a couple of days to see where it settles.

tip Fix those leaks! The U.S. Environmental Protection Agency estimates that 5 percent to 10 percent of American homes have a water leak that exceeds 90 gal. per day. Many of these are cold water leaks, but 90 gal. of hot water a day will cost you between $250 and $1100 every year, depending on your water-heating fuel and utility rates.

◀ Gas water heaters typically don't have actual temperature markings, just general descriptions of "warm," "hot," and "very hot."

▲ The thermostat of an electric water heater usually is marked, but it usually is not accurate. Aim for 120°F, then check the temperature. (Photo by John Curtis.)

▲ Set the temperature as low as you find comfortable, but not less than 120°F. Use a probe thermometer in a glass, and let the water run over it until the thermometer holds steady. (Photo by John Curtis.)

Fixing Leaks

Hot water leaks literally pour money down the drain. Most of us eventually get around to replacing the washers in a leaky faucet, but other leaks are less noticeable.

One leak we may not be so attentive to is the shower diverter, the little push-pull knob in the tub faucet that controls the flow of water to the shower.

Another unexpected "leak," though unusual, is a toilet water supply that is connected to the hot instead of the cold water. Finally, there are heat losses through the walls of your water heater and pipes, both of which can be reduced by adding insulation. I'll show you how.

63 CHECK THE SHOWER DIVERTER

There are three main types of diverters: One is built into the tub faucet nozzle; one is a knob mounted in the wall; one is a lever built into the mixing valve body.

If you have a leaky nozzle-type diverter, either unscrew the nozzle or locate and loosen a set screw near the shower wall at the bottom before pulling off the nozzle. If you have a separate diverter knob, you'll have to pop off the cap and remove the knob screw. Then, pull the knob straight off, and use an adjustable wrench to loosen and remove the packing nut.

Unscrew the valve assembly and pull out the valve. Bring the valve unit or nozzle with you to the hardware store or home center, and match it up with a replacement. (If you find that you have a leaky mixing-valve diverter, get a plumber to help with repair or replacement.)

◄ If water flows out of the tub faucet when you take a shower, you're wasting it. More than a tiny dribble indicates that the diverter valve needs service or replacement.

64 CHECK THE PIPES TO THE TOILET

Occasionally, I see a house that has one or more toilet supply pipes fed with hot water instead of cold water. Some plumbers used to do this to prevent toilet tanks from sweating during humid weather.

If you aren't sure, it's easy to check—turn on the nearest sink or shower until it runs hot, then shut it off. Flush the toilet, and as it refills, check the water supply line with your hand, to determine if it's hot. If so, get a plumber to change the supply to cold—it'll save you a bundle.

65 WRAP YOUR WATER HEATER

If your water heater isn't already internally insulated with foam, and it's not so old that it's nearly ready for replacement, save some energy by insulating the heater with a "tank wrap."

How do you know if your tank has foam insulation? Look at the openings where the pipes emerge from the tank. There is often a plastic trim piece around a pipe fitting that you can slide away from the tank to see if there is yellow plastic foam insulation between the outside metal jacket of the tank and the tank itself. Other places to look include the plastic "button" covers on the tank top and the burner access panel at the bottom. If it's electric, open up one of the thermostat access doors and look at the insulation visible at the sides of the opening. If you see foam, you're good. If all you see is fiberglass, add the tank wrap.

To wrap the tank, you'll need a tank wrap kit sized for your tank. Have handy a sharp utility knife and a tape measure.

Here's how to do it:

1 Start by cutting the main blanket to length. (If you're wrapping a gas water heater, cut the bottom of the wrap about 6 in. shorter than the total height of the tank.)

2 Hold the wrap up to the tank and wrap it around as a test run. Pull it underneath any pipes that run up the side of the tank. If the pipes are too close, you can wrap over the pipes if you have to. If it's too long, mark the vinyl covering, pull it off, and cut the width to fit.

> ▶ Check the size of the insulation wrap first; if it overlaps more than a couple of inches, take it down and trim it to size.

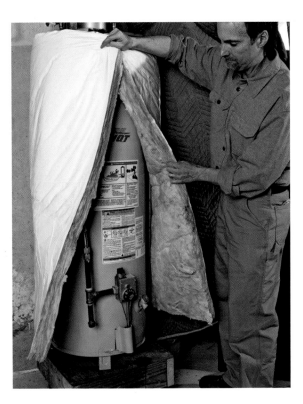

tip Don't waste hot water while you wait. One problem with tankless water heaters as well as with low-flow fixtures is the long wait as hot water fills the pipes between the heater and your sink or shower. Not only does water go down the drain, much of it may be hot water if you're not diligent. A demand-activated hot water circulator (see Resources on p. 116) saves both. Activated by a motion sensor or push button, this system pumps hot water into the supply pipes, shutting off as soon as the water at the tap gets warm. This system is especially helpful with low-flow fixtures and tankless water heaters (see p. 51).

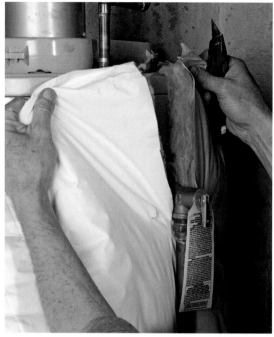

▲ Before getting the wrap in place, you may have to cut a slot for one or more side-mounted pipes. Don't trap the safety valve or discharge pipe behind the blanket.

3 Plan the seam location; if a pipe runs up the side of the tank, try to align the vertical seam with it. If there is more than one pipe on the side, cut a slot in the blanket from the top edge or from the main vertical seam to the pipe location. Don't cover (or bump into) the pressure relief safety valve in the process, and don't cover up the free end of the pipe that exits from the valve.

4 With pieces of adhesive tape ready (about 3 in. to 4 in. long), wrap the blanket around the tank, taping the top edge of the vinyl jacket to the top of the tank in several places. Add a couple more short pieces across the vertical seam to hold it snugly, then tape the vertical seam from top to bottom.

5 For gas water heaters, don't insulate the top because it can be a safety hazard. For an electric tank, cut a slot in the square top piece to slide past any pipes on the top, slip it on, then trim off the extra at the corners.

6 Finish by taping seams on the sides and top. Be sure to cut an opening around any service access panels.

▲ Start installing the wrap by attaching one corner to the top of the tank with a ³/₄-in. piece of tape.

▲ Pull the wrap snugly around the tank and attach it with one or two more pieces of tape.

▲ Use tape to close any slots you had to make to accommodate side-mounted pipes.

▲ Finish the job by neatly taping the main vertical seam, and use any extra pieces of tape to hold down the edges at the top of the tank. Take care not to disturb gas piping. Note the cut-out area for the gas valve, thermostat, drain valve, and burner access. These need to be left accessible.

▲ Access covers on electric tanks should be left exposed. Cut the vinyl in an I-shape with a sharp knife and tuck the flaps in the sides for a neat appearance. (Photo by John Curtis.)

66 INSULATE YOUR PIPES

It's good to insulate all the hot water pipes you can access. Buy enough pipe insulation of the right diameter (usually ½ in. or ¾ in.), making sure to get a little extra. Get a sharp utility knife with a fresh blade and some high-quality duct tape. Wear safety glasses, because it can be dusty overhead.

Here's what to do:

1 Find the hot water outlet pipe at the water heater, and identify where it goes.

2 Start at the corners. Cut the insulation at a 45° angle to make a nice tight joint at each elbow. Use a full length of pipe insulation wherever you can and shorter pieces only where necessary. The insulation is pre-slit along its length, so just slip it on, although you may have to run your finger down the cut to open it.

3 Insulate the straight runs between the corners. It's easier to cut pieces to the right length when they have straight ends. You may need to notch the insulation to fit around floor joists, pipe hangers, or other hardware.

4 At T-fittings, plan for the side of the insulation with the slot to be on the side where "leg" of the T branches off. Cut a hole in the insulation large enough for the "leg" to fit through and install that piece, then butt the insulation on the leg tightly against it.

5 Cut and trim the insulation with a minimum of joints and gaps. If you cut the insulation carefully, you won't need much tape. If you need tape to hold parts of the insulation in place, use a high-quality duct tape, and wrap it several turns around the insulation.

67 energy myth

IF THE OUTSIDE OF MY WATER HEATER DOESN'T FEEL WARM, IT MUST BE WELL INSULATED

Even on a poorly insulated tank, the outside surface of the tank jacket will be pretty close to the room temperature—that doesn't mean you aren't losing a lot of heat. Unless the tank is already internally insulated with foam, it can still benefit from an extra blanket.

▲ At corners, cut a 45° "miter." Using a utility knife, you'll have to cut once from the top and then from the bottom to complete the cut. Long, sharp scissors can also work to make a smooth 45° cut.

▲ Cut your miter so that the lengthwise slot for installing the insulation is at the long or short end of the miter; this makes it easier to slip the piece on.

▲ When estimating the length of a shorter piece with miters on both ends, such as this one, cut it a little bit long. It's easier to trim off extra than it is to add some back.

▲ As you install the insulation, cut around obstructions with a utility knife.

▲ Pull out the excess piece you cut and tuck the insulation over the pipe.

68 TAKING CARE OF YOUR WATER HEATER

tip You can keep a water heater going strong by replacing the anode rod periodically; the anode rod helps prevent corrosion of the tank walls that leads to leaks. This is usually a job for a plumber, but you can do it yourself.

The anode rod is a tube-like length of aluminum or magnesium that hangs down into the tank and, magnet-like, attracts electrically charged particles that otherwise would begin to corrode the tank. To change it you'll turn off the water and the gas or electricity, drain down the tank, and, using a ratchet-type wrench, unscrew the rod from the top of the tank. Take the corroded old one to your plumbing supply store for replacement.

The anode rod hangs inside most water heaters as a "sacrificial" layer that helps prevent corrosion—and eventual failure—of the main tank. (Photo by Charles Miller, courtesy *Fine Homebuilding*, © The Taunton Press, Inc.)

If you have a gas water heater, sediment on the bottom of the tank reduces heat transfer from the burner to the water, wasting energy and money. To clean it out, flush the tank once a year by opening the drain valve at the bottom of the tank wide and letting it run full force into a pail.

You may need to fill the pail a few times, depending on your water quality and the age of the tank. If the tank is older and you've never done this, be careful. If there's a lot of crud in the drain valve, you may have trouble getting it closed once you open it. Find the shut-off valve for the cold water inlet to the tank first, just in case. If the drain valve sticks, you could have a plumber replace it with a new ball valve, or even replace the tank (see the photo below).

69 UPGRADING YOUR WATER HEATER

As with any equipment, it's best to plan for a replacement before your old water heater breaks down. If you wait for a leak, you'll be in hot water and probably will end up with whatever is in the plumber's truck that day, and it won't be the most efficient model.

When you shop for a water heater, look for the highest energy factor, or EF, in a size that suits your needs. For 40-gal. gas water heaters (the most common size), EF ratings start at .58 and go up to .67 (ratings are slightly lower for larger tanks).

Try to find a tank that's .63 or higher; the manufacturer's literature should have this information. Also, ask for a model that has a direct vent or power vent system, which greatly reduces the chance of exposure to carbon monoxide. The Department of Energy is releasing the first ENERGY STAR rating system for water heaters in January 2009, so always look for the ENERGY STAR label.

If you have an electric water heater, look for an energy factor of .93 or better. Or, if you have a gas line to your house, install an efficient gas water heater instead. Standard electric water heaters will not have ENERGY STAR models; if electric is your only option and you live in a warm

▶ Flush out sediment from the bottom of the tank at least once a year. This is another task to do on a Saturday morning rather than a Sunday evening, just in case the valve gets stuck and you need a plumber.

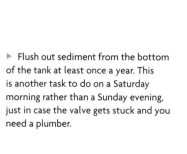

◀ This tankless water heater provides hot water on demand, so there's no heat loss for the 18 to 22 hours a day you aren't actually using hot water. This super high-efficiency model has dedicated combustion air and vents out through the wall—it's much safer than a traditional tank and doesn't need a chimney.

climate, look for an ENERGY STAR heat pump water heater. And, because of their high operating cost, electric water heaters are also typically the best candidates for solar water heating (see the "Go Green" sidebar below).

70 CONSIDER "TANKLESS"

A tankless or instant water heater fires up on demand when you turn on the hot water tap. It's always ready, saving the waste of a standard water heater that's always turning off and on. As with other appliances, the ENERGY STAR label only identifies higher levels of efficiency within each product type—even the least efficient tankless water heaters are more efficient than the ENERGY STAR–rated tank-type units.

Tankless water heaters have much higher EF ratings than tank-type units (in the range of .69 to .85) but are expensive. Choose a unit rated at .82 or higher for maximum savings. The best ones have a variable firing rate to maintain a steady temperature output regardless of how much water you're using.

Be aware of two concerns with tankless water heaters: First, choose one with adequate capacity (rated in gallons per minute) for the uses you anticipate. Some models can provide enough hot water for two showers and laundry at the same time, but some cannot. Second, these units can't produce hot water if the tap is turned on to a trickle, so if you like shaving or rinsing dishes with a tiny stream of water, you will be disappointed. One way to take care of the second issue is to install a small (5-gal.) storage tank and circulator pump.

71 go green

INSTALL A SOLAR WATERHEATER

Solar water heaters are a significant investment ($6,000 to $12,000), but think of it as paying in advance for your hot water. If you have some unshaded roof or wall area that faces near south, a solar water heater can pay rewards for decades. In fact, they are less expensive and offer a faster payback than today's trendier solar equipment, photovoltaic panels (see p. 17). The type and size of the appropriate solar water heater varies depending on your climate, the location of your house, and the size of your family; typically, the collectors are coupled with controls and a preheat storage tank for the best efficiency. (See Resources on p. 116 for information on solar water heating systems and ratings.)

CHAPTER 5

Heating and Cooling

The systems that heat and cool our houses are meant to keep us and our families comfortable, even when weather conditions would make it otherwise. This means that adjusting expectations is an important part of saving energy.

Given our technology capabilities, it's not surprising that we've become accustomed to expect "perfect" indoor environments. Yet "perfect" often translates into houses and offices that are over-air-conditioned in summer and stuffy and hot in winter. So adjusting expectations is an important part of saving energy. You want to be energy efficient both to save money and to save energy. But being energy efficient doesn't mean depriving yourself of comfort. In fact, reducing energy use by addressing problems often improves comfort.

The three main strategies for cutting heating and cooling energy are to reduce the need by making the house itself more efficient; to keep equipment running efficiently through repairs, such as duct sealing, as well as regular service; and to install more efficient heating and cooling equipment when you need to replace those systems.

tip If you wanted to stay warm, you wouldn't put your heater outdoors, but many heating and cooling systems in the United States are partially or completely located in attics and crawl spaces. These harsh environments reduce system performance. It's usually not possible to move the equipment or ducts indoors, but you may be able to move the thermal boundary to include your system. See chapter 7 for more information.

Reduce the Need

Reducing need takes many forms, few of which require doing without. We cover them throughout the book, from sealing and insulating your house to improving the efficiency of your windows (with new double-pane low-e glass, or even applied films). Switching to efficient lighting and appliances, for example, cuts down on waste heat, thereby helping to reduce the need for air-conditioning.

So if you're planning a replacement of your heating or cooling system, it makes sense to make the building improvements first. Then, when you get a new system, it's "sized" for the smaller amount of energy you'll really use so it can work even more efficiently. The remaining tips in this section cover things you can do to further cut the heating and cooling needs of your home.

How Air Moves through Your House

Many houses are depressurized by imbalanced airflow and supply duct leaks, which can cause outdoor air to leak in, or worse: The negative pressure can draw combustion gases and possibly carbon monoxide down the furnace or water heater chimney. Here's an example: Return air gets pulled in by the fan through the central grille in the furnace closet **1** on its way into the open bottom of the furnace **2**. But air is also pulled in through leaks in the platform **3** from places it's not supposed to be: from the garage, through gaps in wall construction **4**, from the attic, through gaps in the top of the furnace closet or wall plates **5**, or from a crawl space **6**, bringing heat, cold, moisture, and fumes along with it. All this air is mixed and pushed through the furnace heat exchanger and air conditioning coil **7**, where it's heated or cooled, and becomes "supply" air on its way to the house; but the story's not over. Supply air seeps out through gaps and leaks in the ductwork **8** into the attic. This air leaves the house, so it acts like an exhaust fan, depressurizing the house. Once air is delivered to the home, any room with a closed door **9** may cause further trouble. If the room doesn't have return ducts, it becomes pressurized, and the higher pressure in the room causes air to leak out through windows **10** or gaps in the wall or attic **11**. Other locations of air handlers and ducts can lead to a wide range of similar problems.

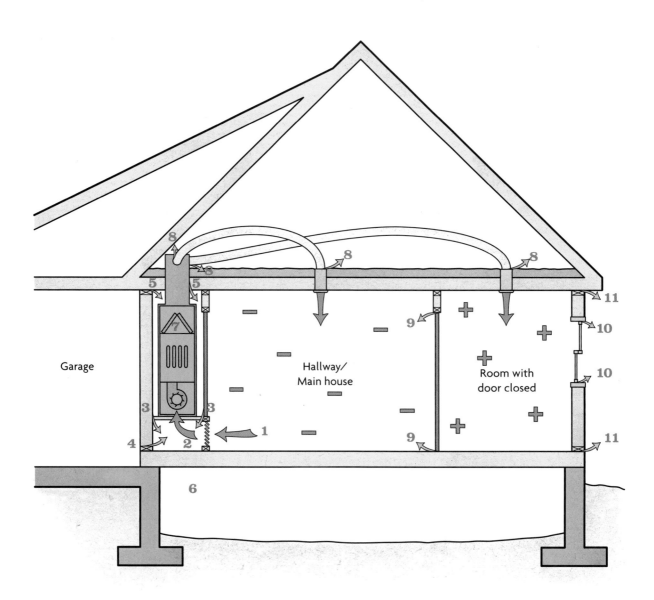

Garage

Hallway/
Main house

Room with
door closed

72 SET BACK YOUR THERMOSTAT

Adjusting your thermostat to a lower setting at night or before you leave home is an easy way to save on heating and cooling needs. It keeps you comfortable and saves you energy.

Of course, if people are home during weekdays, there will be fewer opportunities to turn the thermostat down than if everyone is at work or school on a daily basis. You can set the temperature manually, but many people find it more convenient to use an automatic thermostat.

73 INSTALL AN AUTOMATIC THERMOSTAT

An automatic programmable thermostat doesn't save energy unless you use it. But it will make it more convenient to adjust the temperature on a regular basis. By setting it according to your daily schedule, it can bring the house to the desired temperature a little before you wake up or get home, so you aren't tempted to overcompensate.

I use one that warms up the master bedroom just before bedtime and just before the alarm clock rings, but lets the room run much cooler for most of the night and all day. Today's thermostats are typically pre-programmed, so you have a schedule to start from. I like the units that recognize we have different schedules on weekends: seven-day or "5-1-1-day" models are more flexible. Most units are compatible with the majority of heating and cooling systems, but check the package to be sure. If you have a heat pump or electric resistance heat, you'll need a special thermostat designed for that type of heating system.

74 energy myth

IF I SET BACK THE TEMPERATURE IN MY HOUSE, IT WILL TAKE MORE ENERGY TO BRING THE TEMPERATURE BACK UP

Not true. In cold weather, when the house cools off, the smaller temperature difference means less heat flow to the outside—and that means fewer Btu to buy, even while the house is recovering. (It works exactly the same for air-conditioning, but the temperatures are reversed.) The only time the answer is yes is if you have a heat pump with electric backup heat, or if you are so uncomfortable with the lower setting that you overshoot when you are in the house.

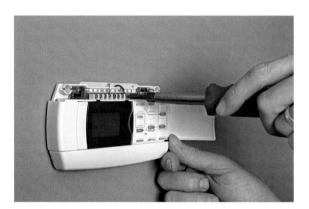

◄ Installing a programmable thermostat for a furnace or heat pump involves low-voltage wiring, which you can do yourself, but you'll want to shut off the power to the furnace before proceeding. Follow the manufacturer's instructions carefully. Depending on your existing heating and cooling system, the thermostat may need a battery to operate.

tip Never use an unvented space heater, even those sold as "vent-free." In addition to the possibility of deadly carbon monoxide gas, unvented heaters generate a lot of moisture and traces of other dangerous chemicals—stuff you don't want in your house.

tip Don't use your fireplace. Of course, a fireplace is great for creating atmosphere, but most wood fireplaces only increase your furnace use. Gas fireplaces perform slightly better, but most are a lot less efficient than a well-tuned furnace.

75 SEAL OFF YOUR CHIMNEY

If you have a fireplace, keep the damper closed when not in use and, if it's rarely used, install an insert that seals much more tightly than a standard damper.

If you want to burn wood, a stove is much more efficient. Pellet stoves have the best user controls, plus high efficiency and low emissions, although you have to purchase bagged "stove chow." In either case, the best choice is a wood or pellet stove with a duct supplying outdoor air for combustion right to the fire box.

▲ If you have a chimney with a standard cast-iron damper, chances are it doesn't close tightly. If you use the fireplace infrequently (or not at all), you can purchase a blow-up chimney damper "stopper" that helps seal it off.

▲ A fireplace "stopper" is not readily visible when installed, so it's important that it has a hanging tag as a reminder to remove it before building a fire.

76 USE A FAN

An automatic setback thermostat helps with air-conditioning too—just be sure to buy one that's labeled "heating/cooling" (some are designed for heating only). But you can also reduce the need for cooling by using fans to stay cool (see p. 36 for information on ceiling fans). Fans only cool you off when you're in the room, however. So unless you use the fan to bring cool outdoor air into the house during the night, don't run it unless you're there to enjoy it. Otherwise, it just wastes electricity and generates heat.

77 SHADE YOUR WINDOWS

The largest single contributor to air-conditioning use in most homes is the sun shining in through windows. And it's not just south-facing windows that cause the problem. For most of the United States, east- and west-facing windows play a much bigger role.

Adding substantial shading to east and west windows can reduce cooling energy significantly without sacrificing the beneficial heat gained from south windows in the winter. Shade the windows from the exterior, or install light-colored, opaque, or semi-opaque shades on the interior.

Adding awnings, a sun shade, or an overhanging deck are all projects that add value to your home and cut your cooling bills at the same time. If you build an arbor or pergola, or if you add trees, you will be reducing carbon emissions at the same time, and plantings allow extra light to reach the windows in winter.

78 INSTALL A WHOLE-HOUSE FAN

Whole-house fans can make a substantial difference in your air-conditioning needs because they bring in cool air at night. Just note that installation may involve an electrician and a carpenter, and will require a ceiling with a vented attic space above it. Also, it's best to install such a fan in a central hall or stairwell.

Choose a unit that has a motorized, insulated cover that seals and insulates the unit when it's not in use. If you already have a whole-house fan, chances are it's very leaky and has no insulation at all, so consider replacing it with a modern unit like the one pictured in the right photo below.

Here's how to use these fans: Keep the windows closed tightly and shaded as much as possible during the day. Then, after the sun sets or before bedtime, open most of the windows in the house and run the fan for 20 to 30 minutes. Run it again in the morning to "flush" out the air in the house and replace it with cool, fresh air, and you're ready to start another day. If you use a whole-house fan properly, you may not need air-conditioning on many days when you normally would use it.

79 energy myth

ATTIC FANS KEEP YOU COOL IN THE SUMMER

Many homes have a fan or two, mounted in the gable end wall of the attic and typically activated with a thermostat so the fan runs when the attic gets hot. Although it may be moderately helpful in cooling off your attic, you don't live in the attic. If you carefully seal air leaks and ducts and insulate the attic, you won't need the fans. Shut them off or disable them by turning the thermostat all the way up.

▲ This old-fashioned whole-house fan is effective at bringing cool air indoors, but it leaks like a sieve all summer and winter—and has no insulation. (Photo by John Curtis.)

▲ A well-designed whole-house fan like this one from Tamarack Technologies has a motorized, insulating cover with effective weatherstripping. (Photo courtesy Tamarack Technologies.)

Keep Equipment Running Efficiently

80 go green

How do you know what filter to buy? Most good-quality filters have a MERV (minimum efficiency reporting value) rating—a higher number means better filtration. Cheap, standard filters don't even have a rating, so look elsewhere. The EPA recommends filters with a rating of 8 MERV or higher, and even 10-MERV to 12-MERV filters are easily available and inexpensive at hardware stores and home centers.

These filters have the MERV rating prominently displayed on the package.

Another key to reducing heating and cooling energy is to ensure that your heating and cooling equipment (furnace, air conditioner, thermostats, and ductwork) operate properly and efficiently.

This involves regular maintenance that you can do yourself, operational changes, repairs such as duct sealing, and proper tune-up service by a qualified technician.

81 USE CLEAN FILTERS

With any furnace or air-conditioning unit, make a point to change the filter once a month when the system is in use. Both heating and air-conditioning systems probably need less attention in the spring and fall, when use is intermittent.

If a filter is really dirty when you change it, change it more often. I've heard people say, "but my filter never gets dirty." This may actually be a sign of a major return-air duct leak that allows air to get around the filter.

It could also mean that there's another filter you didn't notice, perhaps hidden behind one or more return grilles, though that's less likely. If your filter never gets dirty and you know it is the only one, it's a good bet that the interior of your heating/cooling system has gotten caked with dirt, especially the air-conditioning coil (see the left photo below). Have it cleaned, and find and repair the duct leak that's bypassing the filter.

▲ When a filter gets dirty, it restricts the airflow, which hurts your heating and cooling efficiency. Replace it once a month, or when it starts to look like this.

▲ Note the direction of the arrows labeled "airflow." The filter goes on the return side, so the arrows should always point toward the blower compartment or fan. Be sure to put the filter cover back snugly so it doesn't leak.

82 KEEP THE AIR FLOWING

For nearly all furnaces and air conditioners, higher airflow means better efficiency and less wasted energy—so don't do anything that will reduce the flow. Unless you have a problem with a room that receives too much heating or cooling, it's best not to shut off supply-air registers. If you do have a room that's too warm or too cold, your problem may be a duct leak, or it may be simply poor duct design that's restricting airflow.

Once the system has been sealed, it's best to have a professional diagnose and balance airflows in the system (see p. 64). Generally, don't close registers in rooms that you don't use as much. Although it may seem to save a bit, it actually reduces overall system efficiency and may increase duct leakage significantly. Avoid the "filters" that you put in supply registers, because these are just gimmicks.

◀ Keep furniture and clutter away from floor and wall registers—it reduces airflow, efficiency, and comfort. Although the white "register filter" visible inside the grille does not help improve indoor air quality, it is effective at catching crumbs. It's better to leave it out.

83 CLEAN THE COILS

A central air-conditioning system has two coils. If you can get to them, you probably can clean them yourself, although it may be better to leave the job to a technician because getting to them isn't always easy.

The indoor coil (also called the "evaporator" in most systems) is between the furnace and the supply ducts, where it can catch lots of dust, lint, and pet hair in its fins—especially if the filters are in bad shape or there are duct leaks between the filter and the fan.

The outdoor coil (called the "condenser") should be readily accessible. In addition to getting dirty, outdoor coils can be damaged whenever something hits them and bends the fins (the lawn mower, a baseball). Over time, this damage and a buildup of dirt reduces airflow and can cut efficiency dramatically.

The fins are delicate and must stay open to allow air to flow around the coils. It's best to "lift" off the dirt by slipping a "fin comb" between the fins, sliding it behind the dirty or bent area, and lifting the comb teeth out carefully, straightening and clearing dirt as you go. Once clean, coils should be inspected at each tune-up.

▶ When the fins of a condensing coil get mashed or clogged with dirt, air can't flow properly, and efficiency suffers. (Photo by John Curtis.)

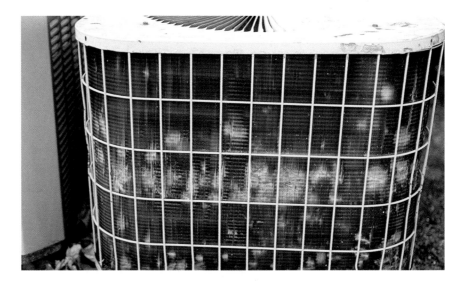

◀ You can use a tool like one of these fin combs to straighten and clean the fins on an air-conditioning coil. Gently slide the comb in, immediately adjacent to the damage or dirt, then carefully sweep it out through the affected area to clean and straighten the metal fins. (Photo by Scott Phillips, © The Taunton Press, Inc.)

▶ A furnace and/or air-conditioning filter slot that has no cover provides a way for dirt to get in past the filter, where it can catch on the coil and reduce airflow. It's also a duct leak that can suck cold air right into your furnace in the winter and leak hot air in the summer. (Photo by John Curtis.)

84 TURN OFF THE FAN

If you currently leave the furnace fan running all day, change the setting on the thermostat to "auto." This alone could save you between $100 and $500 a year on your electric bill. The fan is not intended to run full time, and you shouldn't need to run it 24/7 to be comfortable. A feeling that you need some air moving in the house could indicate one of two things: a need for ventilation (see pp. 34–36), or a comfort problem that can be diagnosed and fixed by a combination of sealing duct leaks (see below) and balancing airflow in ducts (see p. 64).

85 SEAL UP YOUR DUCTS

Sealing your leaky air ducts may be the most important single thing you can do to improve the energy performance of your house. This can be a big project, but it often doesn't require any special skills—just a willingness to crawl into some difficult spots and get dirty.

To find and seal duct leaks, you'll need a gallon or two of duct-sealing mastic (find it at hardware stores or home centers), vinyl gloves, some cheap cotton work gloves, and old clothes or disposable coveralls; it is messy, difficult work. The good news is, once you've sealed the ducts, you shouldn't ever need to do it again. It's a good idea to have some fiberglass mesh tape (available with drywall supplies) and a cordless drill with some sheet metal screws.

First, locate all ductwork in the attic, garage, or vented crawl space. Ductwork in an unfinished basement may be leaky, but sealing those ducts typically won't save much, unless the floor overhead is well insulated and sealed. Shut off the furnace

Efficiency Suffers with Oversized Equipment and Leaky Ducts

Find the rated SEER of your equipment on the top line. This is the ideal efficiency rating. The middle line shows how efficiency suffers if equipment is oversized. The bottom line shows the operating SEER for oversized equipment with leaky ducts.

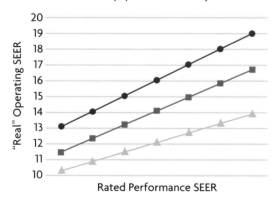

Ideal operation
Oversized equipment, tight ducts
Oversized equipment, leaky ducts

▲ Seal duct connections at the air handler carefully—these are under the highest pressure.

DUCTS MUST BE CLEANED REGULARLY

Unless you've had a big water spill or leak that got into some of your ducts, and as a result there's mold growing inside them, you don't need your ducts cleaned. In fact, the main purpose of duct-cleaning services is to clean out your wallet. Furnaces don't create dust, they just move it around—and any dust that's in your ducts is unlikely to get kicked up if it hasn't already.

or air-conditioning unit at the thermostat, or use the safety shut-off switch; if the unit turns on before the mastic is dry, it can literally blow away your repairs.

The first priority is leaks that are closest to the blower itself, where the pressures are highest. Carefully seal the connections where the largest ducts connect to your furnace or air-conditioning unit, but don't seal cabinet access doors, combustion air inlets, or the filter slot—basically, leave the air handler alone.

Then, work your way down the line, first on the supply side, then on the return. You will likely have to peel some duct insulation away in order to get to the connections; it's important to seal the inner duct material (whether it's sheet metal or plastic flex duct liner) and not just the outside of the insulation jacket. Applying mastic is pretty easy; just smear it in place.

In general, pay attention to the connections between any two sections of duct, especially where a fitting branches from a central "trunk" duct—the connection to the trunk tends to leak badly. Also, the fitting where a smaller branch duct meets the ceiling, wall, or floor (called the "boot") is typically quite leaky; focus on the connection to the duct, to the drywall or subfloor, and to the corners and angles of the boot itself.

▲ First, make a cut in the outer insulation jacket, just enough to expose the leak area. The insulation is black from air leaking through openings in the ductwork.

▲ This duct section was actually broken and needed a couple of sheet metal screws to hold it back together.

▲ Spread a thin layer of mastic on the joints and cut a piece of fiberglass tape to wrap all the way around. If the duct fittings are sturdily attached, there's no need to use the tape.

▲ Next, the tape is embedded in the first layer of mastic and wrapped tightly around the joint.

▲ Once the tape is embedded, thoroughly cover and seal the joints. Notice that the connection of this "takeoff" to the main trunk duct (lower right area) receives a layer of mastic; attached, but no fiber tape.

▲ Once sealed, the insulation is pulled back to cover the duct, and the vapor jacket is repaired with vinyl tape (from www.efi.org/store). You can also use a clamp-type stapler to repair the duct wrap, if it's not badly damaged.

Just make sure you don't seal the chimney or furnace flue connector—it's not a duct. (Furnace flues should be tight and secure, but if you see any gaps, have a heating contractor fix them—never use duct mastic.)

When applying mastic, use a vinyl glove covered with a cotton glove. Then, when you need to use your hands, you can shed the cotton glove and rest that in the pail of mastic. Just put it back on when you're ready for the next spot. Bridge very large gaps with fiberglass tape before applying the mastic.

After the mastic is dry, replace the duct insulation and repair the insulation jacket. Now is the time to insulate any uninsulated ductwork in the system.

▲ Many furnaces are located in a closet in the house or garage, with return grilles in the wall. In addition to pulling air in through the grilles, they also pull in air from your attic, garage, or crawl space; anywhere that openings inside the closet and platform are connected to. (Photo by Terry Brennan, Camroden Associates.)

▲ The solution for a platform return is to line the entire area under the furnace, sealing the joints with mastic and creating an actual return duct. The only openings should be the bottom of the furnace and the return grille(s) or duct(s); these should be completely unobstructed. (Photo by Neil Moyer, Florida Solar Energy Center.)

tip **If your duct system is in an inaccessible area, it's possible to get help from Aeroseal®, an automated duct sealing system, though it may not be available in all markets (see Resources on p. 116).**

◄ A home performance professional can test your ductwork with a special pressurizing fan to see how leaky it is, and recommend fixes. Many can also recommend solutions to comfort problems caused by poor duct design. (Photo © The Energy Conservatory.)

tip Most quality contractors belong to either the Air Conditioning Contractors of America® (ACCA) or the Sheet Metal and Air Conditioning Contractors' National Association (SMACNA) (see Resources on p. 116).
Both organizations provide searchable contractor listings. Also, choose a contractor who is an ENERGY STAR partner, whose technicians are certified by North American Technician Excellence (NATE), or both. Ask whether they test airflow, and whether they use "subcooling" or "superheat" to measure refrigerant charge; if they don't, look for someone else. It's even better if they use an automated system t test the charge.

Pay attention to manners: If contractors can't be prompt and courteous, imagine how they will treat you if they make a mistake and you ask them to fix it. Interview at least two contractors, and don't just choose the one who offers the lowest price. Get references. It is a good sign if they ask about heating or cooling comfort problems you have had and offer sensible explanations and solutions.

▶ A qualified technician should understand how to test your system for refrigerant charge and airflow according to manufacturer's instructions. (Photo by John Curtis.)

Most folks subscribe to one of two philosophies when it comes to servicing heating and cooling systems: Either have it serviced every year whether it needs it or not, or do nothing until it breaks down.

As it turns out, neither one is quite right. Beyond the simple maintenance items you can do yourself, a gas furnace should only need a regular clean and tune every two to three years, or longer if the technician suggests it (oil systems should get a clean and tune annually). Regular service should be limited to cleaning and tuning the blower and coils, gas burner, and vent system, including a thorough inspection of the chimney and the flue connector and checking for flue gas spillage.

When new, or right after ducts are sealed, an air-conditioning system or heat pump should be checked for refrigerant charge and airflow using manufacturer-approved methods; finding and correcting problems here can cut your air-conditioning costs by 10 percent or more. But once it's operating properly, it shouldn't need any additional service of the refrigerant system unless something goes wrong. Many technicians will connect their gauges and "top off" the refrigerant in systems that don't need anything, which can lead to an overcharged system. Don't ask for or allow any other refrigerant service on your system unless you notice performance problems (decreased effectiveness or comfort).

90 INSTALL A CUTOUT THERMOSTAT

If you have a heat pump, install an outdoor cutout thermostat. This inexpensive device shuts down the electric backup heat whenever the outdoor temperature is warm enough that you don't need it. This is especially helpful if you frequently turn the thermostat up and down; without it, the backup heat will run every time you turn the heat up.

If you find that the cutout temperature setting needs to be much higher than 25°F to 30°F, or if there is loss of performance in mild weather, this indicates that something else is amiss with the heat pump or duct system. And don't switch the thermostat to "emergency heat" unless the outdoor unit stops working—which would constitute an "emergency." In that case, have the outdoor unit fixed as soon as possible. That "emergency heat" runs on electric heat only, which costs up to three times as much as heat pump heating.

91 IMPROVE YOUR BOILER EFFICIENCY

If your house is heated with a hot water boiler (you have cast-iron or baseboard radiators), the most important thing you can do is install good controls.

The key to efficient boiler operation is two functions: "cold start" and "post-purge." If you buy a new boiler, insist that it have these capabilities. If you have a relatively new boiler, this control can usually be safely added provided it is re-piped to control condensing.

One benefit of a hot water boiler is its ability to do double duty and make potable hot water for you. But without the cold start and purge, the water heating efficiency suffers in the summer, so these controls will benefit you doubly if the boiler has an "indirect" hot water storage tank. If it doesn't yet, install the indirect tank too, for even better efficiency. Note that these controls do not apply to a steam boiler.

tip **One place you can make a steam boiler system more efficient is around the pipes—exposed basement pipes often leave the basement warmer than the rest of the house! Just be careful; if they are already insulated with old pipe insulation it may contain asbestos, so don't disturb it.**

Asbestos pipe insulation is not dangerous when intact, but if it's damaged or falling apart, it may become airborne and is a risk factor for lung cancer.

With uninsulated steam pipes, a basement can be the warmest room in the house. Insulating them with high-temperature fiberglass, as shown here, helps put the heat where you need it. (Photo by John Curtis.)

Install a More Efficient System

92 energy myth

THE LARGER THE AIR CON-
DITIONER, THE BETTER IT
WILL COOL MY HOUSE

For an air conditioner especially, bigger is *not* better:
Shorter run times mean less
humidity control and more
time spent in the inefficient
startup mode. You will actually get more efficiency and
better comfort if the system
is slightly undersize; the only
drawback could be that you
may not want to wear extra
layers of clothing on the hot-
test days.

Replacing your furnace, boiler, air conditioner, or heat pump with more modern and efficient equipment can be a good investment if your system is older and near the end of its life expectancy.

Plan ahead, however. If you wait until this equipment breaks, you'll have an urgent situation, which doesn't leave you time to be a smart shopper. This is a contractor job, and finding the right contractor begins with the preceding section on finding a service person. In addition, a good contractor won't try to dissuade you from buying high-efficiency equipment. Also, a quality installer should do an independent heating and cooling load calculation, discussed in the following section.

93 GET THE RIGHT-SIZE UNIT

If a contractor wants to replace an existing unit with the same size system, or if he or she gives you a quote over the phone, look elsewhere. Many installers determine replacement equipment size by the size of the current system or the square footage of the house, based on the industry norm. However, the industry norm is to size too large—sometimes much too large. Contractors should do a detailed calculation using "Manual J" or a similar procedure, and they should account for all the energy improvements you've already made.

There is a way you can estimate air-conditioning sizing on your own: Note about how many minutes per hour your present system runs on a very hot afternoon. Divide 60 by that number. So if it's 30 minutes, 60 divided by 30 equals 2 times too big.

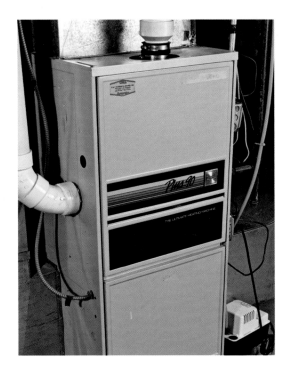

▶ This furnace is so efficient it can vent its exhaust gases through a plastic pipe. Another pipe brings outdoor air right to the unit, making it safer and even more efficient.

94 BUY AN EFFICIENT HEATING SYSTEM

When buying a new heating system, start with an ENERGY STAR label as a minimum; this automatically increases the operating efficiency by about 10 percent over the standard new furnace. Furnaces are rated using AFUE (annual fuel utilization efficiency), and the higher the AFUE, the better.

Another factor that can help save energy is the electrical efficiency of the equipment. The Consortium for Energy Efficiency maintains a list of efficient gas furnaces; go to www.cee1.org and click on the link "Residential Gas Heating" under "Gas Programs" for a list of furnaces that are efficient with both gas and electricity consumption. Generally, a multispeed furnace provides the most electrical savings and quietest operation, because it runs on low speed most of the time.

▲ An efficient furnace or boiler generates so little waste heat, it doesn't even need a chimney. The outside termination doesn't look, or act, much different than a dryer vent.

tip Touted as "free energy" from the earth, geothermal systems (actually ground source heat pumps) are far from free. They may be a good match for superefficient new homes, but with a typical price tag of $20,000 to $30,000, and operating costs that often exceed marketing claims, savings range from a few hundred to $2,000 each year (perhaps as much as $3,000 if you currently heat with oil or electric resistance). If you heat with gas, you'll save more by upgrading your house, and then installing a very high-efficiency furnace and/or air conditioner. If you're considering geothermal, start with an independent home performance consultation to evaluate your options carefully; then look for installers with a track record, and carefully interview past customers.

95 BUY AN EFFICIENT AIR CONDITIONER

For a new air conditioner, the SEER (seasonal energy efficiency ratio) is the rating for efficiency, and the higher, the better. As usual, choose at least an ENERGY STAR–labeled unit.

It's important to ensure that the indoor and outdoor coils are matched for proper operation, and many indoor coils won't work properly with efficient, new equipment. If the installer wants to replace only your outdoor unit, shop around for a different installer; at least get a second opinion.

Refrigerant charge and airflow should also be checked on every new installation, as with an existing system (see p. 64). And as with furnaces, a variable-speed air-conditioning system will provide the highest efficiency of all, by more effectively matching the output to the conditions. A searchable database of high-efficiency cooling equipment is available at www.cee1.org; click "HVAC" under "Residential."

CHAPTER 6

Your Leaky House

You'd think that the biggest leaks in your house happen at the windows and doors. But many of the biggest air leaks are hidden, tucked away in places you would never think to look, like inside your attic, basement, crawl space, porch, and garage.

A house with hidden air leaks can hurt you in a number of ways. Cold air sneaking in makes your house drafty and uncomfortable. Escaping air wastes expensive heat or air-conditioning and carries moisture that can lead to mold or decay. Air leaking through basements, crawl spaces, attics, or garages wastes energy and can carry pesticides, allergens, or even toxic fumes into your home. Sealing large and small holes is one of the best ways to increase the comfort and energy efficiency of your home while saving you money.

Although your attic and basement often have the biggest leaks, these can take some time and effort to seal, so let's start by sealing some of the easier ones. If you have air leaks in the exterior walls of your house, you feel the effects of them every day. Sealing them tight is a relatively quick fix that can help make your house more comfortable.

96 go green

Sealing air leaks not only saves energy and carbon emissions, but it also helps with air quality and building durability—two other cornerstones of green building. By controlling airflow, you control moisture that moves with the air, reducing the chance of condensation that can lead to mold and rot.

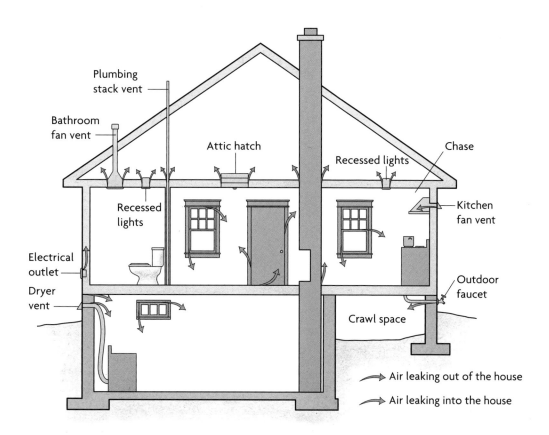

Plumbing stack vent

Bathroom fan vent

Attic hatch

Chase

Recessed lights

Recessed lights

Kitchen fan vent

Electrical outlet

Dryer vent

Outdoor faucet

Crawl space

→ Air leaking out of the house

→ Air leaking into the house

Start **Indoors**

Indoors you'll find two types of leaks. Some leaks are relatively direct to the outdoors, although most are small gaps at the exterior walls. Others connect indirectly to the outside, through openings hidden between walls and floors. In most homes, these are responsible for the biggest leaks, but it's better to try to stop them where they emerge to the outdoors: in the attic, basement, crawl space, garage, or porch. We're going to focus first on the more direct leaks at the exterior walls.

For this work, you'll need a caulking gun, caulk, a soft brush (like a paintbrush or whisk broom), and rags for cleaning up. Generally, you'll use "siliconized" acrylic caulk in visible areas inside your house—it's commonly available in white, brown, or clear, and other colors are available. Unlike 100 percent silicone caulk, you can paint over siliconized caulk to match surrounding surfaces.

To start, look for gaps where window and door trim meets the wall, and where baseboards meet the floor. Once you find a gap, remove any dust or loose debris with the brush. When caulking, push the tip of the tube steadily along as you squeeze the handle, so the material oozes into the crack a bit and also adheres well to the sides. Don't move the tip so fast that you stretch the caulking into a thin string, and don't use it on gaps any wider than $\frac{1}{4}$ in. Excess acrylic caulk cleans up with water before it dries, but it's a good idea to start caulking in an inconspicuous place for practice.

98 **SEAL GAPS AROUND WINDOWS AND BASEBOARDS**

You'll often find a gap where your inside walls meet windows and doors. This gap can let warm air out in the winter and hot air in during the summer.

Let's fix it:

1 Clean the area around the crack with a soft brush or rag.

2 Run a bead of acrylic caulk around the window or door.

3 Using your finger, smooth the caulk into the crack between the wall and the window or door. Do the same wherever you find gaps where the baseboard meets the floor and outside wall.

▲ Many homes have gaps between the window trim and the inside wall—this can allow outside air to pass in and out through the window frame. Caulk any gaps you find between the trim and the wall.

▲ Cut the end of the caulking tube with a sharp knife, at a slight angle, so that the opening of the tube is no larger than the size of the bead of caulk you want (usually less than $\frac{1}{4}$ in.).

99 OUTLETS AND SWITCHES

Outlet and light switch boxes in outside walls are often sources of air leaks. Air often finds its way through these outside electrical boxes, stealing your heat or air-conditioning—and your money. You'll need a flat-head screwdriver and enough foam gaskets (available at any home center or hardware store) to cover all the outlets.

Here's the fix:

Note: To be safe, shut off the appropriate circuit breaker before working on each unit.

1 With a small flat-head screwdriver, remove the cover of the outlet or switch, taking care not to touch or disturb the wiring inside.

2 Remove the cutout(s) from the middle of the foam, and securely fit the gasket over the outlet or switch. For multiswitch or outlet boxes, simply fit a separate gasket over each section, overlapping the edges of the foam.

3 Reinstall the plastic cover.

100 energy myth

INSULATION
MAKES A HOUSE TIGHT

Conventional insulation is like a thick, knitted sweater. Without a wind breaker on top, the air moves right through the sweater—seriously compromising its performance (you get cold!). Sealing and insulation work the same way—you have to put them together to work effectively.

▲ It's easy to remove the covers of electrical outlets and switches and slip a foam gasket underneath to help keep the air out.

▲ An alternative to gaskets: Replace outlet covers in outside walls with a childproof sliding cover that also seals leaks. It's more expensive, but it's great if you have children around the house—no more wrecking your fingers pulling out the little safety plugs.

102 SEALING AROUND THE CHIMNEY

A fireplace surround and chimney can be a big source of air leaks to the outside, even if it's an interior fireplace. It's much better to seal a chimney opening where it exits into the unheated attic (see p. 78), but sometimes that's just not accessible.

If that's the case, you can at least caulk gaps between the masonry and the adjoining wood trim. Again, use siliconized acrylic caulk in visible areas, so you can paint it to match. However, 100 percent silicone caulk is more reliable, if it's out of sight.

101 go green

Anytime you tighten up a house, you have to pay attention to air quality. It's important to ensure that combustion equipment works properly, and that you have an operating ventilation system. (See pp. 34–36 for more tips on ventilation and p. 64 for combustion equipment operation.)

▶ Caulking between fireplace brick and the surrounding trim can slow down the loss of air from your house.

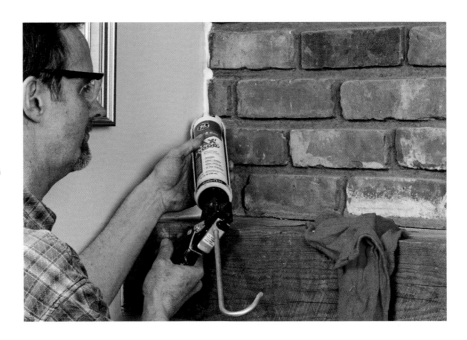

103 RECESSED FIXTURES

Recessed light fixtures are often a source of big air leaks. Most recessed fixtures are vented to dissipate heat, so they must not be covered with insulation or foam sealants. I recommend replacing old recessed fixtures with airtight fixtures that are labeled for insulation contact (or "IC"). These are readily available at home centers—try to get ones that are also rated "airtight."

You'll want to replace each fixture that is exposed in an attic area. You can hire an electrician to replace them, or you can do it yourself. If you want to do it yourself, the simplest fix is to use an airtight compact fluorescent insert (see p. 20) to stop the airflow from the inside.

▲ Have an electrician replace old recessed light fixtures with insulation contact (IC) rated fixtures to seal air leaks around lights. Once you have an IC-rated light fixture, you can insulate right over the top. It's a good idea to use a fiberglass batt here, even if you're going to add blown-in insulation later.

1 Replace the fixture with an IC-rated unit and insert a compact fluorescent bulb, or install an airtight compact fluorescent insert in your existing fixtures (see p. 20).

2 Before reinstalling the trim ring, caulk any gap between the fixture and the drywall ceiling.

3 With and IC-rated fixture, it's also safe to insulate over the fixture from above with some fiberglass insulation.

Take It Outside

With caulk gun in hand, let's head outside. The biggest sealable leaks outside are typically found in overhangs, around doors and windows, and where walls and foundations meet.

104 SEALING OVERHANGS

The first step in sealing leaks around overhangs is to determine what materials you are dealing with. If the bottom of the overhang is covered with vinyl or aluminum siding, probe gently behind it to see if there is a solid layer of wood underneath. If not, your best bet is to have a professional take the siding off and add a continuous air barrier (such as thermoply, $\frac{3}{8}$-in. OSB, or $\frac{1}{2}$-in. rigid insulation) beneath the siding. Removing vinyl or aluminum and getting it back up without damage is tricky; it's best to get someone with experience to handle that. If the bottom of the overhang is plywood or a similar solid material, caulk around the edges to seal the gaps. In visible areas, siliconized acrylic can be painted to match; in an inconspicuous area, 100 percent silicone is more durable.

▲ Overhangs often have significant gaps around the bottom edge that allow cold air into a house through the floor. (Photo by John Curtis.)

▲ This overhang has fiberglass insulation and vinyl covering, but the wind blows right through both. This is roughly the equivalent of hanging a blanket loosely in front of an open window—or, in this house, with 40-ft. overhangs both front and back, the blanket covers three wide-open doors.

105 SEAL THE FOUNDATION GAP

Inspect the bottom edge of the walls where the siding meets the foundation. Look for gaps between the wood sheathing (plywood or boards behind the siding) and the top edge of the foundation wall. Brush out any loose dirt and caulk the holes with 100 percent silicone, pushing the tip of the caulk tube as far into the crack as possible. Any large gaps (more than $\frac{1}{4}$ in.) are better sealed using spray foam—you can trim off any visible foam with a knife after it's fully cured (which usually takes several hours).

▲ There is often a gap where the exterior wall meets a foundation or slab, and caulking from the outside can be the easiest way to address it. Use 100 percent silicone for all exterior caulking that will be out of sight or won't need to be painted.

To the Attic

In most homes, the biggest and most costly leaks—which mean the biggest opportunities for savings—are in the attic or basement. Here's why: Sealing the living area of your house means keeping out air that comes in from any area of the home that's not heated or air-conditioned. In most homes, basements and attics are big, unheated spaces. These two areas are typically riddled with holes from pipes, wiring, ductwork, and even interior wall cavities that are open to the attic and basement.

You don't see these holes from inside your house, but they're there, and they are sometimes big enough to stick your arm into. I've even crawled through some. Attic air sealing is a medium-size project that can take several hours or several afternoons, but it's well worth your time. And it should always be tackled before you cover things up by adding more insulation.

Air Leaks Hide in Your Attic

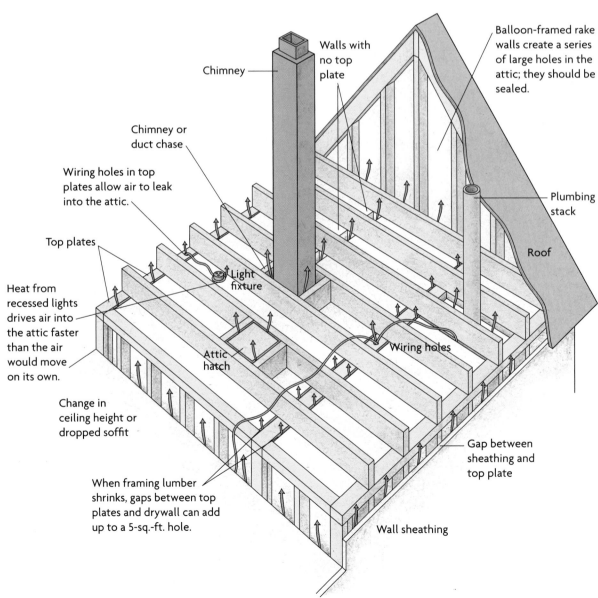

Chimney

Walls with no top plate

Balloon-framed rake walls create a series of large holes in the attic; they should be sealed.

Chimney or duct chase

Wiring holes in top plates allow air to leak into the attic.

Top plates

Heat from recessed lights drives air into the attic faster than the air would move on its own.

Light fixture

Plumbing stack

Roof

Attic hatch

Wiring holes

Change in ceiling height or dropped soffit

Gap between sheathing and top plate

When framing lumber shrinks, gaps between top plates and drywall can add up to a 5-sq.-ft. hole.

Wall sheathing

106 MAP YOUR FLOOR

Walking around the top floor of your house, make a rough sketch of the layout of all walls, including closets. On your "floor plan," note any changes in ceiling height, including ceilings that drop down over bathtubs, vanities, or cabinets. Also note the locations of nonrecessed ceiling-mounted light fixtures—which are typically in the centers of rooms and closets—bathroom exhaust fans, and chimneys. These are where you'll find most attic leaks.

tip The more complex a home's design, the more places air can leak. For instance, every place an interior wall meets an attic or anywhere the ceiling drops or angles down is a likely location of an air leak. Interestingly enough, modern homes with combinations of "tray" and cathedral ceilings, split floor levels, vaulted entryways and great rooms, and complexly-shaped spaces may leak more than an old farmhouse, laid out as a simple box.

A Floor Plan to Understand Your Attic

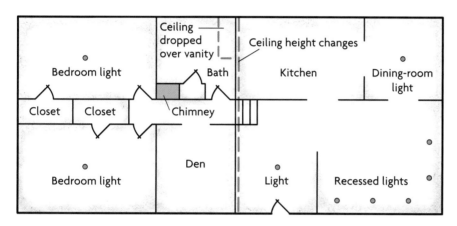

107 INTO THE ATTIC

Take your sketch up to the attic. You'll need gloves, old clothing with long sleeves (fiberglass is itchy), a sturdy flashlight (a head lamp can be very handy), a brush, a utility knife, and a few cans of spray foam. Also protect your lungs. I prefer a fitted respirator, but many people find a dust mask adequate for short-term exposure (an N-95 rating is good for this purpose).

It's worth the extra $40 to buy a foam applicator gun (www.efi.org)—the foam is much easier to control—especially if you have a big attic, or need foam for other projects. Be careful not to disturb electrical wiring or junction boxes. Also, in warm weather, avoid spending prolonged periods of time in the attic during the day because you can dehydrate quickly.

As you move through your attic, identify any dropped ceilings or changes in ceiling height that you noted below on your sketch, along with the tops of the interior walls. The

▶ When you are working in your attic, always be sure to support your weight on the wood beams there or you may crack the drywall (or fall through!). You can place a 12-in.- to 18-in.-wide board or piece of plywood across the joists, and try to keep your weight low and spread out (knee pads can really help). Be sure both ends of the board are supported by joists, so you don't end up on a seesaw.

tops of the walls are usually wood and often have holes for wiring. Note any pipes, chimneys, and ducts that emerge into the attic as you go.

Clear insulation from each opening around one or two rooms at a time, finding the leaks, sealing them up, and moving the insulation back into place before moving on. If fiberglass batts are stapled in place, tear away the facing at the edges. Scoop up blown-in insulation and pile it to the side.

Squirt the expanding foam into the cracks (don't just pile it up). But be careful with cracks around fixture boxes or bathroom fans, because you don't want the foam to squirt into them or the room below. For gaps more than 1½ in. wide, stuff fiberglass in first so the foam doesn't just drop through. Don't touch or try to move the foam until it's dry—it will collapse into a sticky mess. (If you make a mistake, let it cure thoroughly, then cut or scrape it away with a utility knife or putty knife.) Keep the end of the foam gun free of buildup by scraping the sides with a utility knife. Let the foam dry so it's not sticky to the touch (typically about 15 to 20 minutes); you can uncover leaks in the next section while you wait.

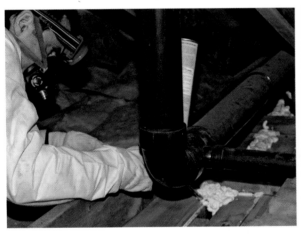

▲ Spray some foam to seal the space between the plumbing vent pipe(s) and the wall framing around it. In this case, there's a double wall that left a gap 1 ½ in. wide by 8 ft. long.

▲ The gaps at the tops of walls may be narrow, but there's a pair along every wall in your house. These can add up to the equivalent of leaving a window open year-round! Seal these gaps while you are plugging wiring and plumbing holes.

▲ Bathroom fans and ceiling electrical boxes, unlike recessed lights, can be sealed to the drywall with foam. Be careful not to shoot the foam into the fixture or electrical box, or through the gap around it.

▲ This fan should be ducted to the outside with an insulated duct. If you're going to replace your bath fan (see pp. 34–35), do that before you seal the gaps. Note the insulation that's black from air leaking.

▲ Some older houses have wall framing that extends right up past the attic floor, leaving the wall cavities open at the top. Once the walls are insulated, you should baffle and seal the openings.

If you can stick your hand down inside a wall, you've identified a hole that needs to be blocked off. Some of these holes occur where the walls below meet the ceiling. In some homes, interior walls can open up right into the attic. Also, where ceiling heights change, there may be no wood blocking between the wall studs, leaving large openings that let air flow freely.

For a large opening, first put down a baffle of heavy cardboard or rigid foam insulation to bridge the gap (1/2-in.-thick foil-faced rigid foam insulation works well). If the opening is in line with the ceiling, it will usually have wood framing at the tops of walls surrounding the opening. If so, cut a piece big enough to cover the hole, plus an extra inch or so. If there are joists crossing over the hole, you will have to cut a separate piece for each section. Brush away any loose dirt and lay the baffle in place. If the openings are between wall studs that extend into the attic, cut a baffle wide enough to tuck between the studs. You may need to stuff a wad of fiberglass insulation into the space to rest the baffle on until you can seal the baffle in place. If the open walls are exterior walls, make sure they are insulated *before* sealing them (see the bottom photo on p. 95).

Once the baffles are in place, use expanding foam around the edges of each piece. Cover the edges with a thick bead that overlaps the surrounding materials by an inch or so. After the foam dries, check for gaps or loose areas, touch up as needed, and replace the insulation on top.

◄ Some air leaks are large enough to stick your head into. Dropped ceilings over attic stairs, boxed-out ceiling areas above cabinets or showers, and spaces where plumbing or ductwork run up to the attic can be a superhighway for unwanted airflow. In this case, the gap is only a few inches wide, but it's 12 ft. long.

◄ A simple fix for most bigger leaks is to cover them with 1/2-in. rigid foam insulation. Set the foam board at the drywall ceiling and wall framing, and seal around the edges with expanding foam.

▶ This one was a tight fit, because of the narrow gap between the plywood flooring and the opening into the wall. It was well worth doing, though, even if it meant ripping up a section of plywood.

tip **If you have an interior closet with a furnace or water heater, don't cover any screened openings that exist between the closet and the attic. These are required by code for combustion air—unless you are replacing the furnace or water heater with a direct-vent system, which is preferred.**

Chimneys require special attention. You can't use flammable materials (like foam) within 2 in. of an active chimney, furnace flue, or water heater vent pipe. Instead, cover gaps between a chimney and wood framing with aluminum flashing.

First, brush away loose dirt on the chimney surface and the wood framing around it. Cut the aluminum flashing to size with a utility knife, using a scrap of wood as a cutting board. The aluminum should be wide enough to cover the space between the chimney and the nearest wood framing, plus 1 in. or so. You'll need a piece for each side of the chimney. Treat very large openings adjacent to a chimney just as you would the extra-large holes (see p. 77). Use rigid foam or cardboard for most of the area, saving the aluminum for the spaces closest to the chimney. Staple the flashing to the wood framing so that the edge touches the side of the chimney. Seal the gaps where the aluminum meets the chimney and the wood framing with 100 percent silicone caulk.

▶ Within 2 in. of a chimney, use aluminum flashing and silicone caulk to seal any openings. Any gaps that are more than 2 in. away may be sealed with foam.

▲ A 2-ft. hole for a 7-in. chimney! And black insulation all around. The black color on the fiberglass insulation isn't mold; it's dust, and it indicates an air leak. Air has been moving through the insulation on its way out of the house for years, and the fiberglass acts like a filter, trapping the dust.

▲ You can cut out the shape to fit the hole, then staple or nail the flashing in place.

▲ Again, silicone caulk seals the openings within 2 in., and foam handles the rest. Note that the hole extended past the truss. In the upper left corner, you can see the $1/2$-in. rigid insulation and foam that was used to bridge that additional gap, just like any other large leak.

A common and often significant leak is found behind kneewalls (the half-height, second-floor attics found in Cape Cod–style houses), finished rooms over garages, and the outside edges of other finished attic spaces. These spaces are usually unheated and vented to the outdoors, and the spaces between the floor joists that run into living space often open wide into this kneewall area. If the space has ductwork, equipment, or pipes, consider hiring a spray foam installer to seal and insulate the entire roof behind the kneewall area. If there is a floor behind the kneewall (often plywood or boards), you can take a similar approach or get a carpenter to cut and temporarily remove an 18-in. section of floor behind the kneewall so you can install the baffles as shown on p. 80.

tip Another reason to insulate and seal the roof line instead of floor spaces is if you use the kneewall space in the attic for storage. If there are multiple access doors or built-in drawers or cabinets, these can be difficult to seal and insulate. In addition to spraying foam insulation on the roof, you may also consider insulating the rafters with fiberglass. Cover the area with 2-in. rigid foam insulation (as shown in the photo below) and seal the seams with spray foam.

Airflow Behind a Kneewall

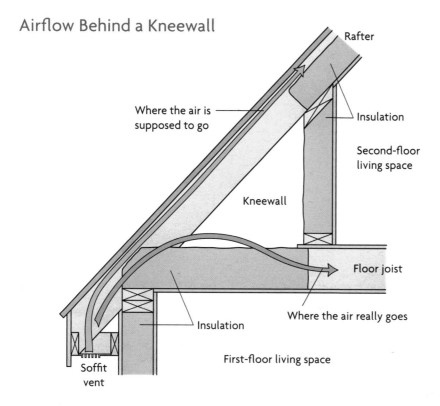

- Rafter
- Where the air is supposed to go
- Insulation
- Second-floor living space
- Kneewall
- Floor joist
- Where the air really goes
- Insulation
- First-floor living space
- Soffit vent

◄ This roof was already insulated with fiberglass batts, but the paper facing does not make a good air barrier, and I wanted more insulation value. The solution was to add 2 in. of rigid foam, held in place with 1x3 wood furring strips. The furring is installed at 12-in. or 16-in. on-center spacing to provide a solid base for installing drywall. (Photo by Randy O'Rourke.)

First, if there's no existing hatch to get into this space, you need to cut an access panel in the wall. Once inside, if you find there is no flooring, just open floor joists, cut baffles of 1-in.-thick rigid foam insulation to fit vertically between each floor joist and at right angles to them, just below the wall. Cut them ½ in. shorter than the distance between the joists and press them in place. Now lay a thick bead of expanding foam around the perimeter of each baffle to seal the gaps and hold it in place.

▶ Once you get inside the kneewall area, look for spaces between the floor joists right underneath the kneewall itself. Unless the rafters above are insulated and sealed, these openings need to be plugged. Typically, the baffles wold be installed right under the wall. In this case, the flooring extends past the kneewall, and I've already insulated under the floored area before sealing the gap.

▲ Cut a baffle of 1-in. rigid foam to fit in each space, and seal around it with expanding foam. While you are foaming around it, the 1-in. foam will stand up and stay put better than the ½-in. foam we've used in the other attic spaces.

▲ Cutting the rigid foam a bit shorter than the space between the joists makes it easy to fit in place and leaves a small gap to spray foam into.

Down in the Basement

When air-sealing the basement, it's tempting to seal and insulate a basement ceiling. However, it's typically better to seal and insulate the foundation walls. If you have a furnace or ducts in the basement, or any finished living space, definitely concentrate on the walls. Generally, the difficulty and cost to treat the walls is higher, but the reward for doing it right is significant.

If your basement is wet, take care of the problem by diverting surface runoff, or add an interior drainage system to handle moisture before tackling the energy problems. See p. 101 for advice on treating basement moisture.

111 SEALING BASEMENT WALLS

If your basement is "inside," meaning that you heat it during the winter, seal the air leaks between the basement and outside. Even underground holes can leak air, depending on the soil, and can bring soil gases (including radon), pesticides, and mold inside. So even if the basement is "outside," it's still a good idea to stop potential leaks at the basement walls. Don't try to seal around the main electrical service coming in because it can be difficult to reach and is a safety hazard. Usually, this is sealed from the outside by the installing electrician. If the outside entrance appears leaky, have an electrician or the power company take a look.

Next, survey foundation walls and the wood sill at the top of the foundation that the first floor sits on. Go all the way around and look for holes where wiring and pipes enter. You may find other gaps where windows and doors meet foundation walls, or anywhere wood framing meets the foundation.

Brush away loose dirt from the surfaces and be sure they are dry, then seal around pipes with silicone caulk wherever they go through wood or concrete. If the gap is more than 1/4 in., foam the gap. If the basement is anything other than solid concrete (brick, mortared or unmortared stone, or cement block), I recommend 2 in. of professionally applied closed-cell insulation on the entire wall, for sealing, insulation, and moisture control (see p. 100). This can take care of the sill area (below) at the same time.

tip Sealing leaks in the perimeter of a foundation doesn't just save energy; it also helps keep pests out. A client of mine reported a 90-percent drop in his rodent problem after spraying urethane foam on the walls and sill of his crawl space. And during the 15 years I've lived in my own pretty-well-sealed house, the only time mice got in was when the door sweep on the basement door broke.

▲ Seal around pipe and wire penetrations at the perimeter of your basement with spray foam or caulking.

▲ Cutting the rigid foam a bit shorter than the space between the joists makes it easy to fit in place, and leaves a small gap to fill with spray foam.

▲ Cut a rigid foam plug to fit the space between the floor beams, and seal around the plugs with expanding foam.

113 SEALING THE SILL

The sill area, where the house rests on the foundation, can be very leaky. Although theoretically you could caulk all the cracks from the foundation up, in practice that's hard to do, because it's difficult or impossible to see or reach these areas, and they are typically encrusted with construction debris and decades of dust. The simplest way to both seal and insulate this area is to use foam board "plugs."

First, remove any existing batt insulation that's tucked into the area. If it's in decent shape, set it aside and reuse it. If not, bag it with the trash. Brush off whatever loose dirt you can reach easily on the top of the foundation wall (wear safety glasses and a dust mask). Then measure the distance between the top of the foundation and the bottom of the floor and cut strips of 2-in.-thick polystyrene foam to that dimension minus ⅛ in. Use a bread knife or a tablesaw (the foam comes in 2-ft. by 8-ft. boards). Cut the pieces to length with a knife, about ½ in. shorter than the distance between the floor joists (see the photo on p. 81).

Cut a notch in each piece for pipes, wires, or other services running to the outside through that space. Don't trap active water pipes (including heating system pipes) between the insulation and the wood because they may freeze in cold weather. If you're not sure, leave it exposed and try to spray foam in the cracks you can reach behind the pipe.

114 SEAL THE BULKHEAD DOOR

Some homes have a bulkhead access into the basement. The metal doors on top keep most of the rain out, but they are far from airtight, and inside them should be a tight, insulated exterior door at the bottom of the steps (if you don't have such a door, have one installed). Even if the door is already there, it's common to find a large gap between the top of the door frame and the nearest floor joist. This should be sealed up with a strip of plywood and caulked around the edges.

▲ With gaps along the door frame that let air and moisture leak through, this bulkhead cover alone is anything but energy efficient.

▲ Inside the bulkhead, an opening over the top of an otherwise tight door can be a big gap. It should be covered with a solid material like plywood, and sealed around the edges with caulking.

115 SEAL THE FLOOR OVERHEAD

You may decide to tackle leaks in the floor instead of the basement walls, because you have no heating equipment in the basement and really want it to be an unheated space. In that case, focus on plumbing, electrical wires, and ducts that go up through the floor from below. Most of these leaks can be sealed at the floor level, using the same techniques as the attic leaks discussed earlier.

If your home has wood planks instead of plywood on the underside of the floor, there can be too many cracks to seal by hand, so you may be better off hiring a contractor to spray the entire floor surface to get a good seal.

To start, make a map of your first-floor walls, noting the locations of plumbing fixtures and chimneys, then, in the basement, find these areas on your map. You may have to pull down some insulation to see what's going on. Always use safety glasses and a dust mask when working overhead. Look for holes in the underside of the floor, whether there's a wire or pipe going through it or not. Seal the holes with foam; larger holes will need a baffle first, tacked in place with a couple of small nails or screws.

◄ Like the attic leaks, you can seal small holes around plumbing or wiring with foam. Plug the big holes with rigid insulation baffles, sealed with foam. Always wear safety glasses when using foam or when caulking overhead.

116 SEALING THE CRAWL SPACE

In general, treat a crawl space foundation as if it were a very short basement (see p. 103). The preferred place to seal (and insulate) a crawl space is at the exterior walls, but, as with a basement, any leaking water should be fixed before proceeding. This approach diverges with the historical tradition of venting these spaces to the outdoors, and for good reason: Venting has been shown to introduce more moisture than it removes, along with ushering outdoor air into your home.

Other Leaky Areas

The other areas where big leaks often lurk are in garages, covered porches, and other attached structures that have their own attic spaces, including any one-story "wing" that you may not realize has its own little attic.

The approach is generally the same for all of these types of structures, and it is very similar to the kneewall project on pp. 79–80. Fixing these leaks can be pretty easy, but like anything else dealing with the home, it can turn into a big job, depending on whether there is easy access to the spaces. Still, it's well worth dealing with these gaps, because they are often equivalent to leaving several windows open. If you're not sure how to proceed, you may want to have a home performance analyst or similar professional to do a more thorough evaluation (see pp. 11–12).

117 SEALING THE GARAGE CEILING

Hidden leaks in the framing between the garage and the house can let garage air into floor and wall spaces, and even allow toxic auto fumes into the house. If you have an attached garage, an open pathway from the garage to your house is a safety hazard and an energy problem.

Whether the garage is on the side of the house or beneath it, the biggest holes are usually where the garage ceiling meets the house. If living space is above the garage, the following process won't work. If the garage is at the basement level, with living space on top, you can access the gaps from the basement, provided the basement is unfinished.

If there's finished space both above and next to the garage, the only way to access the leaks would be to cut away pieces of drywall. In that case, it's better to get a home performance professional to evaluate the magnitude of the problem and suggest possible solutions, which could include cellulose or foam insulation sprayed in through small holes.

For an attached garage, access these gaps from the attic space above the garage. If there's no access panel, hire a carpenter to build you a small access door. Once inside, look where the garage ceiling joists meet the house. If the joists run perpendicular to the house, it may look just like the kneewall on p. 79, with open spaces between each. If the joists run parallel to the house wall, a space may run the length of the garage above or below the joist closest to the house. Pull away any insulation and see if you can find a gap between the joists. In some cases, there will be a small crack that you can seal with expanding foam.

If the gaps are more than an inch wide, cut pieces of 1-in. rigid foam just wide enough to fit the openings. Set them in place, in line with the

▲ Sealing joist spaces between an unfinished basement and a garage can lead to a lot of energy savings, as well as decreasing the risk of carbon monoxide entering the house from the garage.

◀ Fixing leaky floor joists or other openings from a garage attic is much like treating a kneewall—fill the holes with rigid-foam baffles, and seal the edges with expanding foam.

◀ This gap in the wall sheathing communicates with other big air leaks in the house (the dark color shows that air has been moving through this insulation). It's the same wall cavity that's open to the attic in the top photo on p. 77.

▲ In this case, I covered the unsheathed portion of this wall with ½-in. rigid foam—it's the same thickness as the plywood. Then I sealed around the edges with spray foam.

▲ Cover the whole surface of the wall that's exposed in the attic with an additional 2 in. of rigid foam—this will add R-value and help seal it even more. Seal the edges and any gaps in the insulation with more spray foam.

wall that adjoins the house, and seal the edges with expanding spray foam. After it's dry, replace any insulation you moved to get access.

Finally, take a look at the surface of the house wall that's exposed above the joists and below the garage roof. It's probably covered with plywood or boards. You can caulk or foam any gaps in the boards. Another approach, if there are lots of gaps or if there is no plywood or board covering at all, is to cover the whole surface with 2-in. rigid foam insulation, and seal the seams in the insulation with expanding foam. (This will also add to the insulation on that wall of the house.) Hold the insulation in place with 3-in. screws or nails; use "roofing tins" from the home center or small pieces of sturdy cardboard to keep the foam from pulling through the screw heads. Also, spray some expanding foam to seal the outside edges of the insulation to the wall.

118 OTHER GARAGE GAPS

While you're in the garage, look for any wiring, plumbing pipes, ducts, or other services that penetrate through the wall adjacent to the house (and the ceiling, if there's heated space above). Caulk or foam around these, sealing them to the drywall. The one opening you should not seal is a combustion air vent (or two) that may be present if you have a furnace or water heater in a closet between the garage and the house. If that's the case, it's best to have a home performance professional evaluate your options.

119 SEALING PORCHES AND OTHER "WINGS"

Wherever a porch roof or other "wing" of a house joins the main house at an outside wall, the roof is often hiding an "unfinished" outside wall that's covered up by the addition. These unfinished areas often include gaps that range from cracks to large areas of wall with no solid material to keep out the wind.

If a porch attic is big enough to climb into, it's usually a matter of making a temporary access (cutting through the drywall and patching it, or making a permanent access hatch). It may seem like a hassle, but if you have a big opening right into the space between your first and second floors, it could be well worth it. Also, if the first-story wing is heated space, gaining access will offer an opportunity to upgrade the insulation above it as well.

Once in the attic, examine the wall where the porch joins the house, then follow the steps we covered in sealing off the garage. If the space isn't big enough to climb into, or is just a roof with no attic space, there may be options with blown-in or sprayed-in insulation; get a professional to assess the situation for you.

▶ A small added-on roof like this one may be an interesting architectural element, but it can hide some serious air leaks—especially if it's vented. This type of leak is best left to a home performance professional to diagnose and treat. (Photo by John Curtis.)

120 SEAL AND INSULATE HATCHES TO COLD SPACES

Few hatches or access doors into attics, crawl spaces, or other unconditioned areas are well sealed or insulated. That can represent a lot of heat loss. You won't feel a draft from a leaky attic hatch because the warm air is leaking out. Some hatches are made of lightweight paneling that may warp and not sit tightly on the weatherstripping. If yours is warped or lightweight, replace it with sturdy ¾-in. plywood.

1 Cut and install weatherstripping so that the hatch or door contacts it fully when closed. Typically, weatherstripping designed for an exterior steel door (such as Q-Lon®) is inexpensive and works well. If it will be visible, use weatherstripping with a wood or metal base for a finished appearance.

2 Cut a 2-in.-thick piece of rigid foam insulation to fit on the back side of the hatch. If the weatherstripping is on the same side of the door as the insulation (as shown in the top right photo below), the insulation will have to be cut small enough to fit inside the weatherstripping, otherwise the door won't close.

3 Attach the rigid foam to the back of the hatch with 2½-in. screws, using cardboard or fender washers to keep the screw heads from pulling through. Although 2 in. of insulation is less R-value than the surrounding surface, R-10 is a huge improvement over no insulation at all.

▲ Instead of measuring and then cutting the weatherstripping, just hold it in place and mark with a utility knife. Note that the sturdy plywood hatch on the left is already insulated with rigid foam.

▲ Staple the weatherstripping in place all the way around the hatch. Note that the insulation on the back of the hatch (left) is cut smaller than the door, to make room for the weatherstripping.

▶ Attic fold-down stairs are especially difficult to manage effectively—you can't approach them like other access doors because the stairs are in the way. The best fix is to build an airtight, insulated box. This kit (a Therma-Dome attic stair cover, available for $89 at www.efi.org/store) is one of my favorites. The precut kit comes with weatherstripping, foil tape, glue, and even Velcro® tabs that loop around a nail-on cleat to keep it tight. (Photo by John Curtis.)

CHAPTER 7

Insulation

 Insulation is probably the single most important material that contributes to the comfort and energy efficiency of your home. But insulation is often misunderstood. There's more to it than rolling out a blanket in your attic.

Insulation is measured in "R-value," for *resistance* to heat flow. High R-values mean more insulating "power." But R-value doesn't tell the whole story. Insulation has to be installed just right, no matter what kind of insulation you use, to get really good performance. And sealing up air leaks between the insulation and the inside of your house is essential to make sure that the insulation does its job well.

The main areas of your home that need good insulation are the attic or roof, walls, and the foundation or floor. Each area uses different materials and techniques; each is important to the whole. We discuss them all in this chapter.

Insulating Your Attic

In most houses, adding insulation to the attic is always the easiest insulating project, so even older homes have at least some attic insulation. To get the results you want, though, I strongly recommend you seal any leaks into the attic as well as any ducts in your attic before you add insulation, because getting to the leaks is hard enough without adding more layers of insulation to wade through. Adding, and carefully detailing, the insulation you put in should be the last project you do in the attic.

121 ADDING INSULATION

Generally, insulation should be installed on the "floor" of the attic (above the flat ceiling of the living space below), and not at the roof line. One notable exception: Don't invest in the attic floor if you have plans to convert it to living space. I have clients who have added one-third more space to their house by finishing the attic, while significantly reducing their heating bills and increasing comfort on lower floors by sealing and insulating the entire roof with foam.

There are two main ways to add insulation in an attic: insulation *batts*, typically made of fiberglass, or *blown-in* insulation, which is typically made of cellulose or fiberglass. Batt insulation is generally the easiest to install, so we'll cover that first.

122 energy myth

INSULATING 98 PERCENT OF A GIVEN AREA PROVIDES 98 PERCENT INSULATING PERFORMANCE

If you had to wade across a river, would you care about the average depth? Just as the depth of the deepest area would define your success, in an insulated surface (like an attic) the performance of the worst area dominates the overall performance. A gap of 2 percent in an attic insulated with R-38 turns the overall performance into about R-22—a degradation of more than 40 percent.

tip How much insulation is enough? A basic rule of thumb when insulating the attic floor is to end up with somewhere between 12 in. and 18 in. of insulation. If you live in a hot climate, 12 in. is adequate; in a mixed or cold climate, aim for 18 in. In very cold climates, consider up to 24 in. These guidelines will generally lead you to slightly higher R-values than what is typically recommended, but you might as well do it right.

If your attic already has some or no insulation, this is a fairly easy project. To install the batts, you'll need old clothes or a disposable coverall, gloves, a dust mask, and a sharp utility knife.

Here's how to install the batts:

1 Measure the thickness of the existing insulation to see how much you want to add. Most fiberglass is available in 3½-in., 6-in., 9-in., and 12-in. thicknesses, so generally you'll be adding one or two layers of one of those.

2 Measure the attic, calculate the area you need to insulate, and buy the rolls or bundles to meet the requirement. Rolled insulation, with one long piece to a bundle, generally goes faster when insulating a large attic space. Unfaced batts are the best choice here. If you're putting down the first layer (this layer should be kraft-faced), you'll need to know the width of the joist space (usually 16 in. or 24 in.). For the second layer, 24-in.-wide insulation installs more quickly.

▶ Cut the batts to length with a sharp utility knife using the top of a ceiling joist as a base. With thicker insulation, you'll need a straightedge to compress the insulation. (Photo by John Curtis.)

▶ This attic already had 6-in. insulation filling the joists, so we're adding the second layer on top. Be sure the first layer completely covers the ceiling and fills the cavity from side to side and top to bottom.

3 Fill the space between the joists to the top before adding another layer. For example, if your joists are 6 in. deep, and there's already about 3 in. of insulation, add a 3½-in. batt. Then plan your second layer to bring the total up approximately to the recommended level. In our example, in a cold climate, you'd add another 12-in. batt to the resulting 6½ in. for a total of just over 18 in. If the first layer fills the cavity to the top, one additional layer should be adequate, unless you're in a very cold climate.

4 Resting your weight on the joists, or on a board that rests on the joists, be careful not to compress the existing insulation, because that decreases R-value. Start at the edges where there's less head room, and work toward the center. Run the insulation at right angles to the first layer. This helps cover up the wood framing, which has much less R-value than the insulation in between. Try to end up near the attic access hatch so you avoid compressing the new insulation (it's like painting the floor of a room).

124 energy myth

HEAT RISES

Actually, warm air rises. And houses tend to leak, especially at the attic—that's why attics are warmer in winter than they should be. The only reason most people put more insulation in attics than they do in walls is that it is cheaper and easier to put more in the attic, and the myth of heat rising reinforces that thinking. In the summer, cool air sinks, and the upper floor gets hot because the air leaking in is coming from the roof/attic area, where it's superheated. Sealing attic leaks before insulating prevents air exchange in both directions.

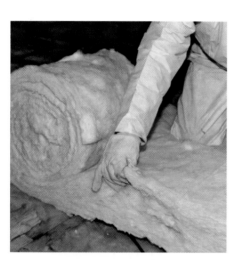

◄ If you don't fluff up the insulation to its full thickness as you unroll or unpack it, you won't get the full rated R-value.

◄ Neatness counts. Be sure to tuck in the insulation as neatly as possible next to the previous batt. Complete coverage is important to achieve the insulation's rated performance.

125 energy myth

ATTIC VENTS ARE FOR
FRESH AIR

**The vents that are typically
installed in attics are *not*
intended to help air flow
through your house, only
through the attic. They
are supposed to help keep
the attic dry, and they do
help. However, sealing leaks
between the house and
the attic is actually more
important.**

126 ADDING VENTS

Attic venting lets moisture escape, preventing it from condensing on cold surfaces in winter. As it turns out, the keys to effective moisture control are thorough air sealing (see chapter 6) and indoor humidity control (see p. 34). Both lower the amount of moisture in the attic. Don't forget that ducts in an attic also may constitute air leaks—if you don't thoroughly seal an attic duct system, you may still have moisture trouble. And be sure to get any bathroom fans vented outside through a gable-end wall or by using a roof cap.

My recommendation is to add vent chutes between the rafters at the eaves edges, and then insulate. Add a ridge vent when you replace the roof, if there isn't one already. And watch the level of attic moisture for the first couple of winters after you insulate. If you don't get any moisture or frost on the underside of the roof, you don't need more vents. If you do, it's always possible to add some combination of ridge, soffit, or roof vents.

▲ Although attic venting is rarely a bad idea, it's overrated. Air and duct sealing and indoor humidity control are much more important. (Photo by John Curtis.)

▲ Foam vent chutes placed against the roof sheathing near the eaves allow a little airspace between the insulation and the roof deck; even if you don't have soffit vents, it's a good idea to install them before insulating. (Photo by John Curtis.)

127 BLOWING IN INSULATION

Blown-in insulation (cellulose or fiberglass) has advantages over batts because it settles and fills in every empty space, providing complete coverage. This quality is especially useful if you have trusses or other obstructions, or if the joist spacing is an odd size, which makes it hard to fit them with batts.

If you want to blow in the insulation yourself, most home centers that sell the loose-fill insulation also rent or lend machines that blow in the insulation.

Here are some keys to a successful job:

1 Be sure there are no loose electrical wires or open junction boxes; in older homes, have an electrician check that there are no active "knob and tube" circuits. Replace all recessed lights in the area to be insulated with new, airtight ones rated for insulation contact.

2 Around chimneys, make a dam of 12-in. fiberglass batts to keep back the insulation.

3 If the attic is floored, remove a strip of the flooring about 6 in. to 12 in. (or the width of one board) around the perimeter of the attic and blow in the insulation.

4 If blowing over a floored area, and there is more than a 3-in. or 4-in. gap between the top of the existing insulation and the floor, fill it with insulation with the hose snaked into the space.

▲ If there are uninsulated sloped ceilings adjacent to the attic, you can insulate them first. Snake the insulation hose down into each rafter space, hold a piece of fiberglass in the opening to keep the material from shooting out in your face, and pull back on the hose as the cavity fills up. (Photo by Bruce Harley.)

▲ When blowing in cellulose, it's very important to wear a dust mask or respirator. Try to get as smooth and complete a blanket of material as possible. (Photo by John Curtis.)

128 INSULATE THE ROOF

Another option for insulating your attic is to insulate the roof—not the floor—of the attic by spraying it with foam insulation. This, however, is a contractor job, not a do-it-yourself project. Another option for roof areas that are already insulated with batt insulation is to add a layer of rigid foam, as shown on p. 79.

If you have a walk-up attic, finishing it off as living space can add value to your home. If you have a furnace or air conditioner with ductwork in the attic, sealing and insulating the roof means you don't have to seal the ducts. But be careful: If your attic contains a chimney-vented furnace, you may cut off the required combustion air. So if you have a furnace inside an insulated attic, make sure it's a modern direct-vent or power-vent furnace. Also, make sure that you fix any roof leaks before adding the foam insulation. It is much more expensive, but the foam not only provides a high-quality insulation layer, it seals the building tightly in one easy operation.

▶ I have had clients who added new living space to their homes by renovating the attic. The most important part of this process is insulating the roof with spray foam. This made their total energy cost bills go down, and they were more comfortable downstairs. Urethane foam may be sprayed directly on the underside of the roof, as shown here, or vent chutes may be added first if there is adequate space. (Photo by Stephen Hill, Air Tight Insulation.)

129 go green

IS IT POSSIBLE TO PRE-SERVE MY ATTIC STORAGE SPACE AND STILL GET A DOUBLE-THICK LAYER OF INSULATION?

Absolutely. But this basically requires adding another floor on top of the existing attic floor by building it up with some 2x6 lumber at right angles to the existing floor joists. The framing should be nailed securely at both ends to perpendicular 2x6s, but be careful not to pinch any wires between the joists. Cover the surface with 1/2-in. plywood or 3/4-in. boards after you insulate the space.

Raising up a floor is the best way to create storage space in the attic without compromising insulation levels. The built-up floor may surround the attic access, or it may be off to one side. (Photo © Kevin Kennefick.)

tip **Stay away from "miracle" products. Foil-faced bubble wraps, layers of laminated plastic, even "reflective" or "radiant" paints—these types of products are frequently sold as having vastly superior performance at a lower price than conventional insulation. Their claims can appear plausible because "radiant" heat flow is hard to understand. But they don't perform; conventional insulation will do the job better at a lower price. If it sounds too good—and too easy—to be true, it is.**

Insulating Walls

tip If your walls already have some insulation in them, it can help to have a home performance professional do an infrared scan to see if there are empty spots or gaps. I've seen "insulated" houses where less than half the walls were ever touched! With guidance from a thermal camera, an installer will know just where to go. Adding wall insulation to an older house that is insulated throughout, but with very thin insulation, can be challenging. It can be difficult to fill the insulation in a consistent, effective way. Find an installer who has experience with older homes and can offer you a good plan to address the situation. Also, have an electrician check for "knob and tube" wiring, which can be a fire hazard near insulation.

Typically, exterior walls contain at least some insulation. And if they don't, it's almost always worth insulating them. The biggest question is how. Should insulation be blown into the wall cavity, or added to the surface beneath the siding? Should you get to it from the inside or from the outside?

If your walls are already insulated, though insufficiently, or if the walls are made of solid material (like stone, block, or brick), the only likely option is to add rigid insulation to the interior (during a remodel) or the exterior (during a residing job). But if you have uninsulated wood-frame wall cavities, the prognosis is good: You have more options.

130 BLOWN-IN WALL INSULATION

This is typically a contractor job, but homeowners can do it, and it can give you excellent results—not just insulating but also making the interior of your home quieter. In most homes, this job is done from the exterior: One or more sections of siding are removed at each floor level around the house, and above and below windows. Holes are drilled into the wood sheathing behind the siding for access to the wall cavities. When the insulation is complete, the holes are plugged, the siding is replaced, and you're done.

Try to find a contractor who has completed a manufacturer-sponsored training program, or who participates in a program such as Home Performance with ENERGY STAR. Always ask for references and also ask about how contractors will patch or refinish the area where they removed the siding or drilled holes. Unless you have vinyl siding (which is easy to move and replace), most contractors will stop short of a paint-grade repair, so you'll have to plan for some surface prep and painting touch-up after the job.

▶ With most types of siding, it's fairly straightforward to remove some of it, drill holes, and fill the wall cavities with insulation. I recommend using a fill tube to reach all the way to the top and bottom of each cavity. (Photo by John Curtis.)

◁ Exterior walls may also be insulated from the inside. This picture shows a nozzle rather than a fill tube. However, it's more difficult to get reliable results with a nozzle. (Photo by John Curtis.)

◁ When blowing insulation into walls, be careful to check for wall cavities that are open into the basement. These may or may not provide an easier way to access the first-floor walls without drilling, but either way, they have to be stuffed with fiberglass to prevent the blown-in insulation from pouring out. (Photo by John Curtis.)

Also talk to prospective contractors about how they find and treat difficult areas and air leakage sites you may not have been able to access. If you have living space over your garage or a narrow attached roof area, have them assess whether insulation can be blown into the garage ceiling or roof. If you can, use a contractor who employs an infrared scan to check their work after the job is complete.

◁ In this attic, the exterior wall cavities are open at the top, and insulation may be easily blown in from above before insulating the attic space. (Photo © Bruce Harley.)

▶ Whether it's in a wall, ceiling, or floor, badly installed insulation doesn't work properly. Take the time to do it right. (Photo by Joseph Lstiburek, courtesy *Fine Homebuilding,* © The Taunton Press, Inc.)

tip Most exterior walls are either 3½ in. or 4 in. deep. Standard batt insulation for a 3½-in. wall is either R-11 or R-13; it's possible to get high-density R-15 batts, but it's a special order in most areas. However, every home center carries R-19 batts. Consider buying R-19 and fitting it into your 2x4 studs, which gives you a total of R-15 after it's compressed. This is even more effective if you have full 4-in. framing, which cannot be filled by standard 3½-in. insulation. You can buy batts in precut bundles, but unless your wall cavity is exactly the right height, you'll have to trim every one to length; buying in rolls may be a better bet. In cold and mixed climates, kraft-faced batts make sense for do-it-yourself projects; in very hot climates, it's better to use unfaced batts.

131 BATT INSULATION

Batt or blanket insulation is very common, is affordable, and is sure to be available wherever you live. It is usually made of fiberglass, but you can also look for rolls of insulation made of mineral wool, or even cotton. It comes in standard sizes based on the spacing of wall studs, or attic and floor joists. It is available with a facing like kraft paper or vinyl that acts as a vapor barrier, but it can also come without. If you live in a hot, humid climate, use unfaced batts. Batt insulation is easy to install in walls if the walls are open, such as when you're renovating or remodeling.

It wouldn't be worth gutting the walls just to add batts. But if you are remodeling any part of the house, make sure the contractor at least installs batts to fill the wall cavity. You may also want to insulate open wall cavities in unfinished areas—for example, uninsulated wood stud walls in a basement.

▶ When cutting batts, measure one and cut it to length. Check it in the wall cavity for proper fit, then use it as a guide to cut the rest of the batts.

Here are the steps:

1 Choose your R-value and insulation type. Measure the square footage of the area and order enough insulation to cover it. Don't worry about deducting for windows or doors unless they amount to more than 10 percent of the overall wall area—it's better to have extra than to run short.

2 Careful detailing is important. Trim the batts properly to fit in odd-sized cavities. Be sure to split the batts over any wires that run horizontally across the wall studs, and tuck the batts in all the way around.

3 Kraft paper facing should not be left exposed, because it's flammable. If you're installing paper-faced batts, they should be covered with ½-in. drywall or plywood as a fire barrier.

132 go green

INSULATE FROM THE INSIDE

Whenever you're adding new insulation to 2x4 walls from the interior, consider adding an inch or two of rigid foam insulation over the studs. You'll have to include wood strips (furring strips) to attach the drywall, so it will cost you a little floor area, but it will save a lot more energy, improve comfort, and make your house greener. Unless you live in the far south, use 2 in. The rigid foam also controls water vapor, so you won't need any kraft facing, and because it's continuous, it effectively negates installation deficiencies and gaps in the cavity insulation.

◄ It's important to take some time to tuck the batts in, so that they fill the entire cavity. Fluff them up before pushing them into the wall, and use a drywall taping knife to tuck the batts into the back corners.

◄ Once the batt is neatly in place, stretch the paper facing over the front of the stud and staple it every 12 in. to 16 in.

**Technically, any layer adds
to your wall insulation. But
the thin, foam backer board
that is typically touted as
"extra insulation" is mostly
to create a flat surface for
the convenience of the siding
installer. The visual impact of
"adding insulation" is better
for customer perception than
it is for their energy bills. Its
real insulating value is less
than R-2, and probably about
R-1 for most products, so I
recommend installing a much
thicker layer (see p. 100).**

The very thin foam backer board
behind most vinyl siding jobs (pink in
this photo) has an R-value between
1 and 2. Although siding contractors
tout the "added insulation," it's really
added for the convenience of the
installer.

134 INSULATION ALTERNATIVES

There are some alternatives for wall insulation you may want to explore. They cost a bit more than batts, but they are worth considering, especially if you are insulating a large area. These fit into two basic categories: sprayed fiber or sprayed foam.

Sprayed fiber is typically either cellulose—usually called "damp spray," because a small amount of water is added (see the photos below and on the facing page)—or fiberglass. These can be sprayed directly into the wall cavity and trimmed, or blown in behind netting or a layer of plastic tacked up to contain it.

Because it conforms to the shape of wall cavities and fills in around any obstructions, sprayed insulation is fairly quick to install. Most important, sprayed insulation gives you maximum thermal performance by eliminating gaps. Although no sprayed fiber can act as an air barrier, higher material densities provide resistance to air currents and also increase the R-value when compared to standard batt insulation.

Sprayed cellulose is also highly flame-retardant, and it can reduce the spread of fire better than other types of insulation. Look for insulation that's treated with sodium borate, a nontoxic fire retardant that also inhibits mold and insects. It's superior to the ammonium sulfate that is more commonly used for fire retardancy.

▲ Damp-spray cellulose is installed just beyond the surface of the wall studs, then scrubbed flat with a rotary brush. (Photo courtesy Green-Stone Industries.)

◄ Damp-spray cellulose fills every cavity completely, easily conforming to every shape and obstruction for a perfect fit. (Photo courtesy Bill Hulstrunk, National Fiber.)

All of these systems work well because they conform perfectly to the insulated space, saving time and labor, while ensuring great performance. The sprayed-on foam products on the market today are the most expensive, but unlike fiber insulation, foam carries the additional benefit of making the space airtight.

Foam typically comes in two densities: $\frac{1}{2}$-lb. "open cell" and 2-lb. "closed cell" foam. Both do a good job of sealing air leaks. Open-cell foam has about the same R-value as the same thickness of cellulose or fiberglass; closed-cell foam has nearly twice the R-value per inch, which is especially valuable in cold climates if your walls are shallow.

► When damp sprayed cellulose is installed, the excess material is scrubbed off so it is flush with the surface of the wall. The extra cellulose that falls on the floor is recycled back into the machine, so it's important that the work site be free of nails, wood scraps, or other trash that could damage the equipment. (Photo courtesy Bill Hulstrunk, National Fiber.)

◄ Sprayed foam can be installed in walls, roofs, and floors. Some contractors offer a 1-in.- to 2-in.-thick spray for air-sealing, followed by a traditional batt or sprayed-cavity insulation to fill the cavity. This approach can be a good value. (Photo by Steve Culpepper, courtesy *Fine Homebuilding*, © The Taunton Press, Inc.)

◄ Sprayed-foam insulation provides an airtight seal wherever it's sprayed and installs quickly. It is pricey; however, it won't shrink, shift, or degrade over the years. (Photo by Stephen Hill, Air Tight.)

135 RIGID FOAM

If you plan to replace the siding on your house, don't miss the opportunity to add insulation, especially if the wall cavities are already insulated or can't be insulated. A layer of foil-faced foam (isocyanurate) under the siding provides the highest R-value per inch and the most benefit in a limited space.

Add the thickest rigid foam you can, while maintaining your existing windows and trim. Typically, this will be about 1 in., depending on the new siding and trim details. Two inches is better for cold climates, but in addition to the added cost of the material, you will probably have to add special trim around windows and doors to accommodate the added wall thickness. If you are replacing your windows at the same time, or if you're in a cold climate and have walls that can't be insulated, do it. The added cost will be worthwhile.

tip If you are adding 1 to 2 in. of rigid foam under new siding, you will want to add ³⁄₄-in. strips called "furring" over the foam board as a solid nail base for the siding. This can be purchased at any home supply store, and should be attached to the wall framing with coated or stainless steel screws.

► If you are replacing the siding on your house, try to have at least 1 in. of rigid foam installed at the same time. In cold climates, 2 in. is preferred, but may involve substantially more carpentry. (Photo by Brian Pontolillo, courtesy *Fine Homebuilding*, © The Taunton Press, Inc.)

Insulating Floors and Foundation

This will be a contractor project for most homeowners, but you can also do it yourself, and the payoff is significant. I prefer to insulate the foundation rather than the floor above the basement because the basement remains usable.

Insulating and finishing a basement wall with standard framing, batt insulation, and drywall poses significant risks, however. Moisture can reduce the insulation's effectiveness and may contribute to mold and rot. So whatever you do, first address water issues (see the tip on p. 102). Yet even when water has been addressed, don't use fiberglass or cellulose insulation against a foundation wall because the inevitable moisture will ruin it. Instead, use sprayed foam to insulate the basement wall, or start with a 2-in. layer of rigid foam against the foundation wall with an insulated stud wall built over it.

136 ADDING FOAM TO A BASEMENT WALL

Installing a 2-in. layer of rigid foam against a stud wall works well if you have a flat foundation wall (either solid or block concrete). Building codes generally require the foam to be covered with ½-in. drywall for protection in case of fire.

An insulated stud wall is the most convenient way to support the foam, and it provides the base for a drywall layer so you'll end up with a nicely finished space. Never install a polyethylene sheet anywhere in this stud wall assembly. The rigid foam provides effective vapor and condensation control.

tip An effective solution for a basement remodel is to cover the floor with a dimpled polyethylene mat, which provides a drainage layer. (See Delta-fl.com for more information on this product.) Every seam and penetration in the mat is sealed carefully, then the floor is covered with 1-in. rigid foam, followed by the plywood subfloor and finished floor. Walls are insulated with 2-in. rigid foam, also taped, and sealed to the dimple mat with spray foam. Then the walls are framed and insulated with batts or sprayed cellulose. To be effective, this dimpled mat should be installed only when there is a floor drain to outside, or a sump pump with a carefully sealed service cover.

▲ This photo shows an effective solution for a basement insulation/remodel as outlined in the tip above. (Photo courtesy Ken Neuhauser)

◀ The basement is shown here before reconstruction. You can even see the water dribbling down the foundation wall under the window. (Photo courtesy Ken Neuhauser)

▲ A shallow surface drain can reduce many wet-basement problems. Dig a trench adjacent to the foundation of the house, 18 in. deep, line it with rubber roofing membrane, install a drain pipe, and fill the trench with a free-draining material like ³/₄-in. washed stone. Top it off with less-permeable soil, such as clay. (Photo by Terry Brennan, Camroden Associates.)

▲ One advantage of a shallow surface drain is that it's much easier to find enough slope to allow the drain pipe to exit above the ground nearby. (Photo by Terry Brennan, Camroden Associates.)

▲ Sprayed foam is an excellent system to use for insulating foundation walls because it seals all the gaps, bonds directly to the foundation wall, and reduces moisture movement. Although it's expensive, I recommend closed-sell foam for underground walls because of its superior moisture control. (Photo by Stephen Hill, Air Tight Insulation.)

tip Here are some key strategies to reduce or eliminate foundation leaks:

1 **Keep gutters and downspouts clear and open, and extend downspouts away from your foundation.**

2 **Ensure that the ground slopes down away from your foundation.**

3 **Avoid overwatering foundation plantings.**

4 **Install a shallow surface drain to drain off subsurface water in (see the top left and center photos above).**

137 INSULATING THE BASEMENT CEILING

I'm not a big fan of insulating the floor over a basement because it typically doesn't result in much savings or improved comfort. But if you don't have a furnace, boiler, ductwork, or heating pipes in your basement, and you carefully seal all air leaks in the floor, it's worth doing. (Use a dust mask or respirator, and wear safety glasses when working overhead. Long sleeves and gloves will help reduce the itching that can happen when working with fiberglass.)

Here's how:

1 Measure your floor and calculate the square footage of the area you need to insulate. Buy insulation in a thickness that will fill (or nearly fill) the floor depth. High-density batts work best; they are typically rated at R-21 for 5½ in., R-30 for 8½ in., or R-38 for 10 in. Buy unfaced insulation in rolls or bundles, and buy enough push rods to cover the area you are insulating at about 24-in. intervals.

2 Gently fluff the insulation to full thickness and press it carefully into place. Cut it to fit neatly around any floor bracing or other obstructions. If wires or pipes run through the floor joists, split the batt and tuck it in around them.

▲ When cutting a batt to length, compress it with a level or straightedge, and cut with a sharp utility knife.

▲ Install the batts in whatever length is convenient for working.

3 Hold the insulation in place with the push rods, about every 24 in. The objective is for the insulation to be snug against the bottom of the floor, but not compressed by the push rods any more than you can help.

▶ Batt insulation in a floor should be held in place with push rods, available at any home center. Insulation should be fluffed up to its full thickness and held snugly against the bottom of the floor.

tip As with any insulation job, if you want floor insulation to perform effectively, you have to take the time to first seal air leaks, then carefully detail the insulation. But remember: If you live in a cold climate, your basement will be quite chilly in winter if you do a really thorough job of insulating the floor.

138 INSULATING YOUR CRAWL SPACE

You may never think much about it, but a crawl space can be a big source of moisture, mold, insects, and other vermin, because most are built with little or no attention to drainage. And usually outside air vents are installed in hopes that any moisture will escape. Scientists now understand that these techniques are ineffective.

A simple way to seal up a crawl space vent is to cut a piece of 1-in.-thick rigid foam insulation the size of the vent and hold it in place with some spray foam. This should only be done in conjunction with a complete crawl space treatment: wall insulation, vapor control on the floor, and water drainage.

The best way to treat a crawl space in any climate is as if it were a short basement, even if you never go down there. Install rigid or sprayed foam on the walls as discussed above, and permanently seal up any outdoor vents. Also, completely cover the floor with plastic sheeting (unless you already have a concrete slab), and include a drain to daylight from the lowest point. If your property is too flat to install a drain, consider installing a sump pump.

▶ This crawl space has insulated walls and an effective, tough polyethylene vapor barrier on the floor to keep moisture out. All seams in the insulation and vapor barrier are carefully sealed, except for the floor drain at the lowest spot (not visible). Depending on the local codes in your area, you may need to cover the foam with a fire barrier, as described on p. 101. (Photo by Bruce Harley, © Conservation Services Group.)

CHAPTER 8

Windows and Doors

 Windows and doors have a tough job to do. Keep the weather out and let air and light in, but not too much. Let us see out, but don't let the neighbors see in. Let people and pets in and out every day, but leave unwanted visitors at the door.

Windows and doors are typically the worst-performing part of your house from a heating and cooling perspective, but when you consider all the things we ask them to do, they still offer a lot of value. And south-facing windows can pay their rent in energy dividends by providing free heating in the winter without adding much to air-conditioning costs in the summer. Windows also reduce the need for electric lighting.

This chapter will help you understand what to look for when replacing windows and doors, and show you how to keep your existing units working as efficiently as possible.

tip Better-performing windows will improve your comfort, because they have an inside surface that's closer to room air temperature, reducing both the surface temperature effect and the "ghost draft."

Energy-Efficient Windows

Buying windows that significantly exceed the building code's minimum requirements helps increase their benefits and minimize their costs over the long haul. Nevertheless, windows are expensive. Despite the persistent claims of replacement window companies, it's rarely worth replacing windows based on energy savings alone.

However, the added cost for good-performing windows is much smaller if you are replacing windows anyway—whether you are doing a complete remodel or just upgrading to a more modern look and feel. We'll discuss things to look for if you buy replacement windows, and also examine some of your options for improving what you already have.

▶ If you are having replacement windows installed, buy the most efficient units you can find that meet your other needs. (Photo by John Curtis.)

tip Upgrade your windows before you replace your air conditioner. By reducing the solar heat gain coefficient (SHGC), low-e glass could save you money twice: by reducing the size of your new air-conditioning system and saving on your cooling bills. Your air-conditioning contractor will have to do a proper sizing calculation for your new system (see p. 66).

How Low-e Glass Works

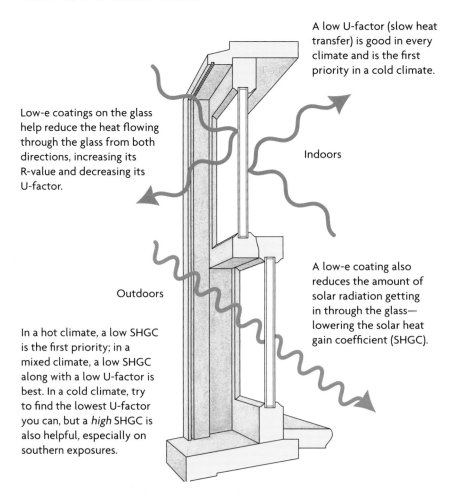

A low U-factor (slow heat transfer) is good in every climate and is the first priority in a cold climate.

Low-e coatings on the glass help reduce the heat flowing through the glass from both directions, increasing its R-value and decreasing its U-factor.

Indoors

A low-e coating also reduces the amount of solar radiation getting in through the glass—lowering the solar heat gain coefficient (SHGC).

Outdoors

In a hot climate, a low SHGC is the first priority; in a mixed climate, a low SHGC along with a low U-factor is best. In a cold climate, try to find the lowest U-factor you can, but a *high* SHGC is also helpful, especially on southern exposures.

Ghost Drafts Occur Even When the Windows Are Tight

The air near the glass is chilled by the cold surface and falls (it's heavier than the room air). When it bounces off the windowsill, you feel a draft. The cold surface of the glass just adds to your discomfort. A window with a lower U-factor will reduce both of these effects and increase your comfort.

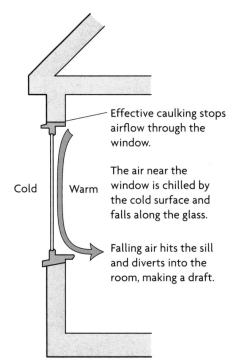

Effective caulking stops airflow through the window.

The air near the window is chilled by the cold surface and falls along the glass.

Cold   Warm

Falling air hits the sill and diverts into the room, making a draft.

139 REPLACEMENT WINDOWS

Here's an old joke: A year after replacing the windows in an elderly woman's home, the window company was still trying to get her to pay up. After many letters went unanswered, somebody finally called the woman to ask about payment. "Payment?" she replied. "But your nice salesman said these windows pay for themselves."

Sadly, windows are just too expensive to pay for their own replacement in reduced energy costs, unless your existing windows are in very rough shape. Fortunately, there are lots of reasons to replace windows other than energy savings: aesthetics, use, ease of cleaning, and comfort. Also, good-quality replacement windows generally enhance a home's value.

The trick is to get the best-performing units you can afford when you're replacing them anyway. An ENERGY STAR label should be an absolute minimum, but current ENERGY STAR window requirements are not much better than code requirements. However, the Department of Energy is proposing some improvements in ENERGY STAR requirements for adoption in 2009, and more dramatic improvements in 2012.

tip Another feature to look for in new windows is a "warm-edge spacer." Rather than using heat-conducting stainless steel to hold the edges of double-pane glass together, more manufacturers are using composites with improved adhesives that conduct less heat.

tip Get "gas-filled" windows. Filling the space between the panes of a low-e window with argon or krypton gas helps lower the U-factor even more. Don't worry about the gas leaking out—it will remain effective until the window edge seal fails, at which point you will have to replace the glass anyway.

▶ Virtually all new windows have performance ratings that consider a number of factors—there are more important choices than "plain" or "insulating" glass. The most important factor in cold climates is the U-factor. U-factor is a measure of heat flow, equal to the inverse of the R-value, and the lower the U-factor, the better. In the south, aim for a low solar heat gain coefficient (SHGC). For mixed climates, a combination of both ensures the best performance.

Window Performance Ratings and Recommendations by Climates

Climate	Very Good		Best	
	U-factor	SHGC	U-factor	SHGC
Cold	.28–.32	*	.10–.27	*
Mixed	.33–.36	.36–.40	.28–.32	.30–.35
Hot	.40–.55	.28–.33	.30–.50	.10–.27

140 GET HIGH-PERFORMANCE STORM WINDOWS

tip In hot climates, don't buy storm windows. Applied solar-control window films or solar screens will do a better job of reducing heat gain, at a lower cost.

Years ago, when all standard windows were single-pane glass, storm windows were the only way to improve window performance in cold and mixed climates. Storm windows don't do much to reduce solar heat gain, though, which is far more important in southern states.

If your existing single-pane windows are in good shape, consider buying a good-quality storm window with a special low-e coating. Although not available from every storm window manufacturer, low-e storms work about as well as double low-e replacement windows, at fraction of the cost.

141 energy myth

USE LOW-E, EVEN ON THE SOUTH SIDE

There's a myth that in cold climates, clear glass is better on the south; the theory goes that double glass without low-e coating is a net benefit because of the increased solar gain. In reality, most northern climates have lots of cloudy winter weather and short days, so the lower heat flow of low-e glass is a net gain. Solar gain is reduced, but the lower heat loss is better for all the hours the sun isn't shining.

142 UPGRADE YOUR EXISTING WINDOWS

Windows are a concern in historic preservation. In some historic districts, replacement windows are not even an option, because it changes the character of the house. And even for an unregulated property, there can be significant heritage value in good-quality wood windows—do you really want to throw that nicely crafted, yellow-pine sash in a Dumpster®? It really can't be replaced.

If you have nice old windows, consider hiring a trained contractor to upgrade them. They can replace the glass on-site with double-pane low-e glass, and take care of weatherstripping and sealing (see the photo at left). As an alternative, you may be able to get hard-coat low-e storm windows or panels fitted to the style of your windows; either approach can meet historic preservation guidelines.

For the best possible performance in a cold or mixed climate, do both. At that point, you will end up with performance that far exceeds current codes, at a lower price than triple-glass high-performance replacement windows.

Bi-Glass® is a window-restoration system licensed to contractors across the country that can be used with virtually any configuration of windowpanes. It allows your existing wood windows to be upgraded to double low-e, with good-quality weatherstripping and tilt-out sash, while preserving the heritage and quality of your existing windows.

▶ Many homes in cold climates already have a storm window covering single-pane primary windows. Note that if the main window has more air leakage than the storm, moisture will accumulate between the windows in cold weather and form condensation (or even frost) on the inside of the storm window. You can reduce or eliminate this by installing effective weatherstripping on the prime window sash. (Photo by John Curtis, courtesy The Taunton Press, Inc.)

143 ADD WEATHERSTRIPPING TO OLD WINDOWS

Older double-hung windows are famous for being loose and leaky. If yours are, it's worth tightening them up. Don't buy rolls of felt weatherstripping because that's ineffective and hard to install. I like the pre-formed V-shaped type shown in the photo below; it's inexpensive and easy to work with. Some other types come in a roll you fold yourself before installing. These work the same way but are not as sturdy as pre-formed V-shaped weatherstripping, though they can fit effectively into narrower gaps.

Here's how to install this type of weatherstripping:

1 Cut a piece to length with a pair of scissors, but don't peel off the paper strip on the sticky back. Open the window sash as much as possible, and be sure the window frame surface is clean and dry. Slip the V-strip in until the free end just lines up with the bottom (or top) of the window frame.

2 Peel about 4 in. of the paper strip off the adhesive backing, press the end of the V-strip into the window frame, then gently pull the paper strip up and out, at a slight angle. When you get to the point where the sash is in the way, keep slipping the paper strip out, pulling gently; see if you can sneak it out all the way to the top. If the paper tears, don't worry, because the last few inches of the V-strip are always hidden behind the window.

3 Do one side, then check the window operation. If the window is not too loose, one side may be all you need. If it's still loose, do the other side. If it's a bit tight, apply a small amount of pure silicone spray lubricant.

4 Press the adhesive backing into place, peel back the exposed flap of the V, and staple it to the window frame. Start at the bottom and work up, being careful to keep the back of the V-strip flat against the window frame so it doesn't buckle.

5 If you see gaps at the bottom of the window or where the two sashes meet, attach a V-strip to stop it up. The bottom piece can be attached right to the bottom of the lower sash; to attach a strip to the middle rail, push the top sash down and the bottom sash up to expose the bottom edge of the upper window. You may find that a narrower (½ in.) V-strip fits better here.

tip **LET THE SUN IN** Whether you have single-pane windows with storms or double-pane windows without storms, remove screens on the south side in the winter—they reduce the solar gain by 10 percent to 15 percent. And keeping the windows clean will maximize solar gain.

tip Using drapes, shades, or rigid insulation panels at night will help make your windows much more efficient and will keep you more comfortable. But be careful: Unless you make a tight seal between the interior covering and the window, you may find a lot of condensation on the window in the morning.

▲ V-shaped vinyl weatherstripping is my preference for loose double-hung windows. After cutting the piece to length, open the sash and slip the strip into the space.

▲ Start peeling the backing off the adhesive near the free end, and work your way up.

▲ A few staples to attach the back of the V-strip to the window frame will help keep it in place for the long term.

144 ADD SASH CORD PULLEY COVERS

Pulley covers are a solution for older double-hung windows. This is not a big energy saver, but if you have a lot of old windows, it can make a difference and also improve your comfort.

Here's how to do it:

1 Be sure the weight ropes are in good shape before you start. Although you can remove the pulley cover to replace the rope later, it's easier to change the rope now if necessary. Now, check for fit to make sure the cover sits flat over the pulley. If it's too low, the cover will ride up on the pulley; if it's too high, you may not be able to get the screws into the wood below the base of the pulley. Sometimes the pulley base is just too wide, and you have to decide whether to trust the adhesive by itself, or just give up.

2 Once you determine that the cover fits your window pulleys, peel off the paper backing and press the cover into place. It helps to thread the little tabs over the sash rope first, then slide the cover up over the pulley.

3 Line it up before pressing the adhesive into place, then screw it firmly to secure.

▲ Peel the paper off the adhesive backing, and slip the small tabs at the bottom of the pulley seal over the rope. Don't press the adhesive into place until you're sure the cover will sit flat.

▲ Attach the pulley seal to the window frame with the screws provided.

tip Temporary storms, also known as "renter's storm windows," don't look nice, but they work. They seal up the leaks and add another layer, decreasing the heat loss. Most people immediately think of shrink-to-fit plastic storms; I prefer a reusable product such as Tyz-All™ window insulating systems (available from www.efi.org/store). These can be taken down and reinstalled year after year. The best quality of all of these products is that they are cheap, costing less than $10 per window.

145 CAULK STORM WINDOWS

Storm windows offer another layer of glass, which nearly doubles the R-value, and they can also help stop air from moving through. If there are large gaps at the edges of the window frame, where it attaches to the house, they should be caulked. However, you don't want the storm window to end up more airtight than the main window, so be sure to weatherstrip the main window first if it needs it.

▲ When caulking around storm windows, leave the weep holes at the bottom clear; if water doesn't drain, the windowsill will rot. Generally, it's not a good idea to caulk around the outside edges of the window trim on the exterior. (Photo by John Curtis, courtesy The Taunton Press, Inc.)

Better Doors

Doors aren't as much of an energy drain as windows. They generally have a little more insulating value, and, most important, there just aren't as many in your house.

Often, the biggest problem with doors is air leaks. However, most of the leakiest doors I've seen were never intended to be exterior doors. Usually they were interior doors, made without any provision for weatherstripping at all. These are often found between the house and garage, or connecting to a walk-up (or walk-in) attic space. Often, it's not even practical to replace them with proper exterior doors. But these doors may benefit greatly from a good door sweep and weatherstripping kit. This fix can improve your comfort, as well as save energy.

146 ADD A HINGED DOOR SWEEP

I've seen so many door sweeps that get caught on an uneven floor, carpet, or threshold that I typically use a hinged "automatic" sweep that flips up ½ in. as the door opens. It's a little harder to find, but worth the effort in the long run. Hinged sweeps can be located online from CRL (www.crlaurence.com) or Macklanburg-Duncan (www.efi.org/store).

Here's how to install one:

1 Measure the distance between the door stops and subtract ³⁄₁₆ in. to ¼ in. Slide the rubber edge out—you'll cut that to length separately later. Mark the location for the cut on the metal part of the sweep, and plan to cut off the end that faces the hinge side of the door so the cut end won't show when the door is open. Cut the sweep to length with a hacksaw, then close the door and hold the sweep in place to make sure it's not too long.

▲ The stops on this door were angled, and too narrow to add weatherstripping over, so I removed them before starting, which changed the length of the sweep.

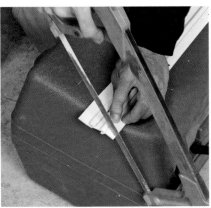

▲ Cut the sweep ³⁄₁₆ in. to ¼ in. shorter than the space it fits into, so it doesn't bind when you close the door.

2 When it fits, slip the rubber edge back into its slot and trim to length with a sharp utility knife. Using a Vise-Grip® or long-handled pliers, squeeze the aluminum track on each end so the rubber edge won't slip out over time.

3 Measure the distance from the door threshold to where the top edge of the sweep will be and follow the instructions that come with the door sweep for the correct dimensions. Make a pencil mark at each end of the door.

4 Close the door and hold the sweep in place so the top edge lines up with the markings. Hold it in place with a screw in the middle; make sure that there's a gap (around ⅛ in.) between the sweep and the door stop, on the latch side of the door. If it's too close, the sweep may bind. Put a screw in through the holes closest to each end.

5 With the door closed, push down on the hinged edge of the sweep to seat it firmly against the floor or threshold. Place the plastic closing button against the door frame or stop near the top of the lower, hinged section and drill a small pilot hole for the longer screw that will hold it in place. Open the door and attach the button with the screw. Verify that the sweep works by opening and closing the door a couple of times, then install the rest of the screws.

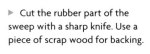

▶ Cut the rubber part of the sweep with a sharp knife. Use a piece of scrap wood for backing.

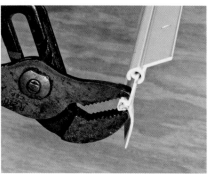

▲ Crimp the ends of the sweep over the rubber edge to hold it in place.

▲ Locate the button that pushes the hinged section, and start a pilot hole; once the hole is just started, open the door slightly and carefully straighten out the drill. In this case, I left a short piece of the original door stop to hold the button, because the rest of the door frame was too far away. The remainder of the stop will be replaced by the weatherstripping kit.

148 WEATHERSTRIP YOUR DOORS

If your exterior door is in decent shape, but the weatherstripping is falling apart, pry the old strips out of the little notch that holds them in place. Replacement strips that fit the same notch are readily available at home centers.

For doors that were never meant to be exterior doors, you'll need to install a new weatherstripping kit. My favorite is a vinyl-covered, spongy V-shape (such as Q-Lon®, available at www.efi.org/store or in home centers), with a metal or wood backing strip. Metal kits are available in brown or white; wood kits are usually brown, with clear or primed wood.

Here's what to do:

1 Depending on the size and shape of your door stops, install the weatherstripping over the stops, or remove the stops and replace them entirely with the weatherstripping. Another consideration is how much room there is between the doorknob and the stop; sometimes, the extra $3/8$-in. to $1/2$-in. thickness is too much, making it necessary to remove the stop.

2 Measure the top strip first, then cut the piece $1/8$ in. shorter than the space. Cut through the metal (or wood) carrier with a hacksaw (or handsaw) and cut through the flexible part with a sharp utility knife. Now close the door and hold the strip in place against the door to compress the flexible section by $1/8$ in. or so. Install two to three screws (or nails) to hold it in place.

3 As you fasten the strip, compress it slightly so it presses fully against the door without pressing so hard it interferes with the door closing. If working with a wood-backed strip, don't drive any nails home until they are all tacked in place and you check the door operation. For metal strips, screws should be installed through adjustment slots. Open the door and install the rest of the screws or nails so the piece is held firm and straight.

tip An even better way to improve your interior garage door is to replace it with a new, insulated steel exterior door. This will save energy, improve your comfort, and help with safety: Many existing interior doors don't meet current fire safety codes for garages. Look for a door that has a 20-minute fire rating, or check with the supplier to make sure the new door meets the applicable code.

▲ When weatherstripping a door, cut the top piece to length and install it first.

4 Measure the strip for one side from the top edge of the top strip to where you want the bottom to end—in this case, above the top of the sweep. Cut the piece about ⅛ in. shorter than your measurement. Be sure you cut the correct piece for the side you measured, because the length may differ. If using a metal-backed strip, the flexible seal needs to be notched to meet the top piece; a wood-backed strip should have one end of the wood carrier already trimmed to fit the top piece neatly.

5 Install the side piece as in step 3 and repeat for the other side. Check carefully for door operation and fit before nailing a wood-backed strip in place.

▲ Cut a V-shaped notch in the upper end of the soft weatherstripping so it will fit neatly with the piece at the top. You can do this with a sharp utility knife; the metal back already has one corner cut off to fit.

▲ After notching the upper end of the weatherstripping, measure the side of the door jamb down to the point at which you want the weatherstripping to end. In this case, it will end just above the hinge of the door sweep.

▲ Then, cut the bottom end to length. Be sure to cut the piece that fits the side of the door you just measured—the door may not be square.

▶ Now, install the side piece. Note the notch at the top end fits neatly against the top piece.

149 UPGRADE YOUR EXTERIOR DOOR

Hundreds of styles of exterior doors are available, and most are just fine.

Here are a few things to look for when replacing an exterior door:

1 Thermal breaks. Many metal-clad doors are filled with insulation, but the frames are solid metal and conduct a lot of heat. Find a door with a "thermal break" in the frame, to cut the heat loss and winter condensation as well. Look in the manufacturer's literature or specifications for that feature.

2 Better glass. Many doors come with a small- to medium-size window, or one or more "side light" panels of small windows. Most are plain double-pane glass, but some doors are available with low-e. Don't spend as much time shopping around for the door specs as you do for windows, but if you have the choice, get the low-e glass.

3 When installing a door, be sure to seal around the frame with low-expansion foam or caulking. Wait until after the door is hung and you know it fits and operates properly (but before the final trim goes on around the frame), then seal it up.

◂ Seal the gap between a door frame and the wood studs with low-expansion foam. Be careful not to squirt too much foam in at once; if the gap is large, too much foam can push the frame out of shape. Wait an hour for the foam to set, and touch up any gaps with some more. (Photo by John Curtis.)

150 GET A STORM DOOR

A storm door will also save energy, although not as much as you might imagine, unless your main door is in really bad shape.

A new, insulated door can be more effective, and it is easier to use and maintain. Always, look for good quality. One thing to avoid is a storm door with a big glass panel, if it's installed over an insulated door on the south, west, or even east side of your house. Unless it's on the north side or well-shaded, the sun shining through the glass can make the insulated door hot enough to badly damage or warp it.

Resources

Publications

Insulate and Weatherize, Bruce Harley,
The Taunton Press, 2002 (www.taunton.com)

EEBA/Building Science Builder Guides (climate-specific
versions); also Water Management Guide, Ventilation
Guide, and Insulation Guide (www.buildingsciencepress.
com or www.eeba.org/bookstore)

General/comprehensive home energy efficiency information

www.energystar.gov (ENERGY STAR consumer links:
Products, Home Improvement, and New Homes)

www.aceee.org/consumer (American Council for an
Energy-Efficient Economy; has good general and
comparison shopping information)

www.eere.energy.gov/consumer/your_home (U.S.
Department of Energy)

www.ase.org/section/_audience/consumers (Alliance to
Save Energy)

www.ornl.gov/sci/btc/pdfs/homeownerguide15.pdf (Oak
Ridge National Lab homeowner fact sheet)

www.bestofbuildingscience.com/videos.html (Oklahoma
State Energy Office: building science videos)

www.finehomebuilding.com (a searchable database of
construction and remodeling information)

Online energy self-assessments

http://hes.lbl.gov (U.S. Dept of Energy/Lawrence
Berkeley National Laboratory)

www.energystar.gov/index.cfm?fuseaction=home_energy_
yardstick.showStep2 (ENERGY STAR Home Energy
Yardstick; or go to www.energystar.gov, click on "Home
Improvement," then click on "Home Energy Yardstick")

"Green living" information

www.nrdc.org/greenliving
(Natural Resources Defense Council)

www.simplesteps.org (Natural Resources Defense Council)

www.greenerchoices.org (Consumer Reports; offers
comparison shopping information in some categories)

www.greenbuildingadvisor.com (Building Green)

www.greenhomeguide.org (U.S. Green Building Council)

www.thegreenguide.com (National Geographic)

www.fightglobalwarming.com
(Environmental Defense Fund)

Comparison shopping information for efficient appliances, electronics, or equipment

www.cnet.com has published comparisons of HDTV
power consumption and lists of the most efficient TVs in
their tests—search for "TV Power Consumption" to find
the latest updates.

The Consortium for Energy Efficiency maintains lists of
very efficient appliances that generally exceed ENERGY
STAR specifications:

www.cee1.org/resid/seha/seha-spec.php3 (home
appliances)

www.cee1.org/resid/rs-ac/rs-ac-main.php3
(heat pumps and air conditioners)

www.cee1.org/gas/gs-ht/gs-ht-main.php3
(gas furnaces and boilers)

www.cee1.org/gas/gs-wh (gas water heaters)

Green/renewable power and carbon offset information

www.green-e.org (Green-e lets you search for renewable
energy and carbon offsets by state and type.)

www.cleanair-coolplanet.org (Clean Air–Cool Planet)

Certified professional energy assessments

www.resnet.us (Residential Energy Services Network—find certified Home Energy Raters)

www.bpi.org (Building Performance Institute—find certified Building Analysts)

Weatherization assistance

These sites offer information on federal, state, and utility assistance for income-qualified consumers, on a state-by-state basis:

www.eere.energy.gov/weatherization/state_activities.html (U.S. Department of Energy)

www.liheap.ncat.org/sp.htm (U.S. Department of Health and Human Services; offers profiles of each state's weatherization programs; also see www.liheap.ncat.org/referral.htm or 866-674-6327 for the department's National Energy Assistance Referral)

www.aarp.org/makeadifference/gettinghelp/articles/energyguide.html (AARP State-by-State Guide to Energy- and Weatherization-Assistance Programs)

Tax credits and other incentives

www.dsireusa.org (The Database of State Incentives for Renewables & Efficiency is a comprehensive directory of federal and state tax credits and incentive programs for energy efficiency and renewable energy. The listings include loan programs, utility programs, tax incentives, grants, and rebates, as well as regulations and corporate/industry incentives, so choose your state and select "See Homeowner Incentive Summaries Only" to get to only the ones you can use.)

www.energytaxincentives.org/consumers (The Tax Incentives Assistance Project website is a good source for summary explanation of federal tax credits available to consumers for energy efficiency and renewable energy activities.)

Also check the websites of your state energy office and your local electric and gas utility companies.

Whole house electric monitors

www.diykyoto.com (Wattson meter)

www.bluelineinnovations.com (PowerCost Monitor™)

www.theenergydetective.com (TED® The Energy Detective™)

Plug-in electric monitors

www.p3international.com/products/special/P4400/P4400-CE.html (Kill A Watt™, Kill A Watt EZ)

www.wattsupmeters.com/secure/products.php (Watts up?)

Lighting design

www.ibacos.com/hpl1.html (Integrated Building and Construction Solutions: High Performance Lighting Guide)

www.lrc.rpi.edu/researchAreas/residential.asp (Rensselaer Polytechnic Institute: Lighting Research Center)

Tubular skylights

www.tru-lite.com (Tru-Lite)

www.odl.com (ODL®)

www.solarindustriesinc.com (Solar Industries Skyview® Skylights)

www.solatube.com (Solatube® Daylighting Systems)

www.sun-dome.com (Sun-Dome®)

www.sun-tek.com (Sun-Tek® Skylights)

www.sunpipe.com (SunPipe®)

www.veluxusa.com (Velux® residential skylights)

Household air quality and healthy remodeling resources, including lead, radon, and asbestos information

www.epa.gov/iaq (U.S. Environmental Protection Agency; asthma, mold, and radon)

www.centerforhealthyhousing.org/html/homeowners.htm (National Center for Healthy Housing; lead)

www.buildingscienceconsulting.com/resources/homeowner.htm (Business Science Consulting; offers "Read This" booklets on healthy home renovations, asthma, and everything you need to know about mold)

Ventilation equipment

www.tamtech.com (Tamarack Technologies whole-house fans and ventilation equipment)

www.fantech.net (Fantech ventilation fans and systems)

www.fancycler.com (FanCycler; information on residential ventilation using air handler and controls)

www.venmar.ca/Home.aspx (Venmar® ventilation equipment and controls)

Weatherization and ventilation supplies

www.efi.org/store (Energy Federation Incorporated; CFL recycling, CFL-wired light fixtures and bulbs, air and duct sealing and weatherization supplies, ventilation equipment, lighting and ventilation controls)

www.conservationtechnology.com (Resource Conservation Technology; efficient building supplies)

www.sheltersupply.com (Shelter Companies; efficient building supplies and ventilation equipment)

www.positive-energy.com (Positive Energy Conservation Products; lighting, ventilation, air sealing)

www.jrproductsinc.com (J&R Products; insulation machines, accessories, sealants)

Duct sealing

www.aeroseal.com (Aeroseal automated duct sealing system; licensed contractors in more than 20 states)

Heat pump water heaters

www.airgenerate.com (AirGenerate™ AirTap™)

www.aers.com (Applied Energy Recovery Systems E-Tech water heaters)

www.nyletherm.com (Nyle Special Projects Nyletherm-110 Heat Pump Water Heater)

www.trevormartin.com (Trevor-Martin Hot Water Generator)

Instant/tankless water heaters

www.boschhotwater.com (Bosch)

www.foreverhotwater.com (Rinnai®)

www.geappliances.com/energy_efficient_home (GE®)

www.noritz.com (Noritz®)

www.takagi.com (Takagi)

Hot water demand and recirculation systems

www.grundfos.com/Web/HomeUs.nsf/Webopslag/PAVA-53MKRN (Grundfos® timer system)

www.lainginc.com/howhot.htm, www.lainginc.com/facts_to_know.htm, www.lainginc.com/act303.htm (Laing Thermotech, Inc. Autocirc1® timer system)

www.gothotwater.com (Metlund® D'MAND® system)

www.taco-hvac.com/en/products/D'MAND System/products.html?current_category=362 (Taco® D'MAND system)

www.uponor-usa.com/Header/Service/For-Professionals/Products/DMAND.aspx (Uponor D'MAND system)

Pool pump sizing information

www.eere.energy.gov/consumer/your_home/water_heating/index.cfm/mytopic=13290 (U.S. Department of Energy)

www.powermat.com/pools/pumpsize.html (Hot Sun Industries Inc. "Sizing the Pool Pump")

www.discount-pool-supplies.com/pump-sizing-guide.php (Discount Pool & Spa Supplies "Notes on Pool/Spa Sizing")

www.poolplaza.com/pool-pump-sizing-2.shtml (Pool Plaza "Pump Sizing")

Heating and cooling systems contractors

www.natex.org/consumer_locator.htm (North American Technician Excellence; third-party certification)

www.acca.org/consumer (Air Conditioning Contractors of America; membership organization)

www.smacna.org/directory (Sheet Metal and Air Conditioning Contractors' National Association; membership organization)

Insulation

www.sprayfoam.org (Spray Polyurethane Foam Alliance)

www.dow.com/styrofoam/na/thermax/whychoose.htm (Dow® Thermax™; rigid foam rated for exposed service)

www.cellulose.org/members_producer.html (Cellulose Installation Manufacturers Association; manufacturer links can provide contractor referrals)

www.naima.org (North American Insulation Manufacturers Association)

Insulation installation and training

http://cec.ishow.com/mod/index.cfm?ModCon=cein&SubCon=buen_res&TxtModCon=cein_txt (California Energy Commission; cellulose)

http://cec.ishow.com/mod/index.cfm?ModCon=fiin&SubCon=buen_res&TxtModCon=fiin_txt (California Energy Commission; fiberglass)

www.owenscorning.com/around/insulation/installitright.asp (Owens Corning®)

www.ccpnetwork.com (CertainTeed)

Solar energy— hot water and electricity

www.nrel.gov/rredc/pvwatts (National Renewable Energy Laboratory; solar electric calculator)

www.fsec.ucf.edu/en/consumer/solar_hot_water/index.htm (Florida Solar Energy Center; objective information on solar thermal collectors and pool heaters)

www.solar-rating.org (Solar Rating and Certification Corporation; ratings of solar water heating and pool heating collectors and systems)

www.findsolar.com (Find Solar; solar system estimators and links to local installers)

www.altenergystore.com (Alternative Energy Store; information and retail sales)

www.realgoods.com (Real Goods; solar and alternative energy products)

www.solardirect.com (Solar Direct; information and retail sales)

Window restoration/efficiency upgrade system

www.bi-glass.com (Bi-Glass Systems)

Low-e storm window manufacturers

www.alliedwindow.com (Allied Window Inc.)

www.cityproof.com (Cityproof®)

www.harveyind.com (Harvey® Industries Inc.)

www.stormwindows.com (Innerglass Window Systems)

www.winstromwindows.com (Winstrom Windows)

Solar-control window films

www.cpfilms.com/windowfilms.html (CPFilms Inc.)

www.3m.com/US/arch_construct (3M®)

Index